A Twin-engine Pilot in WWII

Robert F. Hornbeck

Here's to blue skies and happy landings.
Bob Hornbeck

PublishAmerica
Baltimore

© 2003 by Robert F. Hornbeck.
All rights reserved. No part of this book may be reproduced in any form without written permission from the publishers, except by a reviewer who may quote brief passages in a review to be printed in a newspaper or magazine.

First printing

ISBN: 1-59286-711-1
PUBLISHED BY PUBLISHAMERICA BOOK PUBLISHERS
www.publishamerica.com
Baltimore

Printed in the United States of America

ACKNOWLEDGMENTS

I would like to acknowledge the support and encouragement of my dear wife and to thank her for her many valuable suggestions as I struggled to put this all together. She has inspired and challenged me. Without her love and her patience, it would have been a lesser accomplishment.

I also want to thank my good friend Clarence Hoenig for providing information about PublishAmerica and encouraging me to publish this account of my wartime experiences.

To all “who love the vastness of the sky”

-- Army Air Corps song

HIGH FLIGHT

Oh! I have slipped the surly bonds of earth
And danced the skies on laughter-silvered wings;
Sunward I've climbed, and joined the tumbling mirth
Of sun-split clouds--and done a hundred things
You have not dreamed of--wheeled and soared and swung
High in the sunlit silence. Hov'ring there
I've chased the shouting wind along, and flung
My eager craft through footless halls of air.
Up, up the long, delirious, burning blue
I've topped the wind-swept heights with easy grace
Where never lark, nor even eagle flew-
And, while with silent lifting mind I've trod
The high untrespassed sanctity of space
Put out my hand and touched the face of God.

Pilot Officer JOHN G. MAGEE, JR.
American flier with the Royal Canadian Air Force.
Died in aerial combat on December 11, 1941

CONTENTS

Preface

Several years ago I started writing my recollections about being an aviation cadet and pilot in World War II. My goal was simply to get down on paper some of the things I experienced, particularly for my grandchildren who might some day wonder what it was like back then. I remember reading recently an account by an author about his uncle, who was also in World War II. He had been told never to ask his uncle about the war and his uncle never talked about it. After years had gone by, he decided to ask him about it and was fascinated by the uncle's stories of what he had experienced. Finally, he asked his uncle why he had never told any of these stories before. The answer was short, but revealing. He simply said, "Nobody ever asked me!"

I'm glad that I persisted and have finally completed the writing. I describe briefly some of the events leading up to World War II as I experienced them and the challenges and excitement of being accepted into the Army Air Force as an aviation cadet in 1942; going through flying school and getting my pilot's wings; serving as a B25 instructor pilot; and finally, training in the Douglas A20 Havoc for combat in the Pacific. I have tried to minimize the technical details, but I did amplify on a few things that were important to understanding what was happening in some of the anecdotes. In fact, as I think of it, that's all that it is, a series of anecdotes strung together with a thin narrative. But then, to a certain extent, that's what life is, except without the narrative.

Prologue: my first flight

Curtis JN-4 Jenny

One day in July 1927, my father, mother, and I (at the tender age of three-and-a-half years) were out at the flying field at 79th and Western Avenue in Chicago to watch the airplanes. A well-known cross country flier and barnstormer by the name of Charles Beaulieu (or Ballou) was there offering to take people up for rides in his two-seat biplane (a war-surplus Jenny). The response from the crowd was singularly silent -- there were no takers. Finally, he noticed me standing nearby with my parents and said that he would take the youngest boy there and his mother up for a ride free, gesturing to my mother and me. She deferred to my father, however, not feeling particularly enthusiastic about the prospect. Knowing what he was about, the flier insisted that it be the mother, not the father, so she consented and off we went. Needless to say, when we returned safely with broad smiles on our faces, business picked up considerably.

I could say that this was the beginning of a lifelong desire on my part to become a pilot, but that would be highly imaginative. I have no direct recollection of the experience -- only the induced memories from having heard my mother tell the story over the years.

1
Early experiences on my way to flight training

Prelude to war

My earliest recollections related to the events leading up to World War II are those involving radio news broadcasts and occasional Movietone news clips shown at the Saturday afternoon matinees at the local theater. I recall hearing about the Italians moving against Ethiopia in 1935 and seeing newsreels of Italian planes bombing Ethiopian tribesman. (In those days, we called it Abyssinia.) Although I was only eleven at the time, it seemed a grossly unfair and uncivilized thing to do. I was not able to appreciate the fine points of international politics and aspirations to national glory at that tender age; as I grew older and wiser in the ways of the world, it became clear how truly barbaric and despicable it was.

Hitler's rise to power and political machinations in the 1930s were frequently in the news, but seemed far removed from our personal lives and the struggle to "make ends meet" in the depression years. German occupation of the Rhineland in 1936, the German-Austrian "Anschluss" in 1938, and the pressure on Czechoslovakia to yield the Sudetenland at the Munich Conference in September 1938 were all prominent in the news and in my consciousness. I recall quite clearly the newsreel shot of Chamberlain returning triumphantly from that ill-fated conference as he stepped off the plane, waving the infamous treaty and proclaiming "peace in our time." I also recall my boyhood hero, Charles Lindbergh, returning from Nazi Germany in 1936 with dire predictions of Hitler's growing air armada and the increasing military strength of his regime. "Lindy" was not too popular for voicing such sentiments and lost a little of his luster for associating too closely with the Nazis. The fact that he was presented with a medal by the German government on his visit in 1938 didn't help.

During this period (my preteens and early teens) I was very much interested in aviation. For me, it took the place of sports, in which I had very little interest. I made model airplanes of the most popular fighters of World War I and collected and traded the equivalent of "baseball cards" with my friends that had pictures of and data on the principal aces of the war: Eddie Rickenbacker, Frank Luke (the "balloon-buster"), Rene Fonck, the top French ace, Billy Bishop, the top Canadian, and of course, the "Red Baron," Manfred von Richtofen. I avidly read a monthly magazine called "Flying Aces" which contained many fictional stories about flying as well as accounts of actual flying experiences of the greats and the not-quite greats. (The reference above to World War I reminds me that a columnist recently wrote that there was nothing designated as World War I until World War II had occurred. Until then, it was simply known as the Great War.)

My first awareness of the possibility of war in the Pacific came from reading a story in "Flying Aces" in 1937 of a war occurring in the distant future of the 1940s between the United States and Japan. We were familiar with Japan's aggressions in Manchuria and China, but it was much farther away and more remote than even Ethiopia or Europe. The possibility of us being in a war with a nation so distant, and with a great ocean between us, seemed almost too difficult to comprehend at the time. The fact that within a few short years I, myself, would be participating in such a war was virtually inconceivable.

However, the mills of the gods were grinding on. The announcement in August of 1939 of the non-aggression pact between the Soviet Union and Nazi Germany was, itself, virtually inconceivable. It was a shrewd move on Hitler's part, giving Stalin permission to occupy lands that he would soon take back from him, thereby keeping him out of the war Germany was about to initiate in Poland. On September 1st, the other shoe dropped and the world was once more at war.

The year 1940 was my senior year in high school. (I was in the mid-year class, running from February of one year to January of the next. Thus I graduated from elementary school in January 1937 and from high school in January 1941.) The war in Europe was much in the news, with stories of Dunkirk, the fall of France, and the air war against Britain. Movies such as "Eagle Squadron" and films of the RAF in combat excited my imagination and intensified my interest in flying. I resolved that if we became involved in the war, I would try for flying school. While in high school, I spent four years in the high school ROTC. I had no illusions about military life and particularly about being involved in a ground war as a "ground-pounder." At that point in my life, I had two major goals: to get a degree in chemistry and to learn to fly. The former was attainable, the latter appeared to be only a forlorn hope.

Pearl Harbor

For many of my generation, the words "Pearl Harbor" express not a place but an event. Few of us have actually been to Pearl Harbor, I haven't myself, but all of us experienced it. It has been said, quite rightly, that two events occurred in our lives that were so vividly impressed on our memories that we shall always recall where we were when we heard of them. One is the attack on Pearl Harbor on December 7, 1941 and the other is the assassination of President Kennedy on November 22, 1963.

Although the attack on Pearl Harbor occurred sixty-one years ago, I can visualize the room in which I was sitting on that fateful Sunday afternoon, doing my homework in chemistry while listening to the radio. (I can almost remember the problem I was working on; it had something to do with the volume of gas generated when so many grams of material X react with compound Y to produce etc., etc.) Suddenly the enormity of what I was hearing pushed everything else out of my consciousness. Japanese air attacks against our fleet, against the airplanes at Hickam Field, against Schofield Barracks, thousands of casualties, it went on and on. This imitation nation with its imitation airplanes, imitation ships, "Made in Japan" a hallmark of cheap, shoddy merchandise, had done the impossible. They had carried out a fabulously successful air raid thousands of miles from home and inflicted potentially disastrous damage on our fleet and forces in the Pacific. Due to administrative foul-ups not known to the American public for many years and well depicted in the movie "Tora! Tora! Tora!", it was characterized as a sneak attack, a "date that will live in infamy," as so aptly expressed by President Roosevelt. Nothing in the mind of man was more successful in rousing a lethargic public to the threat of war and to united action. Very quickly, we learned that far from being cheap imitations, their military aircraft and naval ships were highly successful and capable weapons of war.

At the time I was a member of a young people's group in the Grand Crossing Covenant Church on the south side of Chicago. We met every Sunday afternoon at 5 p.m. before the regular Sunday night worship service. The talk that afternoon was of the war and who was going to join what. There was a military draft for young men of age 20 and above, but I was still only 17 (my 18th birthday was in sixteen days), and most of my friends in the church group were about the same age. Nevertheless, in the first flush of excitement over our country being at war, we talked with great enthusiasm of joining the Marines, the Army, the Navy, the Coast Guard, etc., on into the evening.

The next day, reality hit. I wanted to get into a flying program but the lower age limit for the aviation cadets was 20; there was also a requirement for two years of college. I learned that the army did have flight training for enlisted men that led to becoming a sergeant-pilot, but one had to have parental permission to get into the program. No way could I get my parents' permission for such a venture and so it was not a very real possibility for me.

After several weeks, it was announced that 18-year-olds would have to register for the draft on June 30th, 1942. At the same time, the age limit for aviation cadet training was lowered to 18 and the college requirement was eliminated. At last I had a chance! I convinced my parents that if I didn't join the Air Corps, I would end up being drafted into the infantry and would have to slog out the war on the ground (an activity for which I was eminently unqualified).

By the middle of May, I found myself in a hot, stuffy room in one of the government buildings in downtown Chicago, sweating over a written exam with 74 other hopeful applicants. Taking written exams was my meat and potatoes, as I had always done well scholastically. I was at the top of my high school class and had practically straight As in my first year of college. Therefore, I was not surprised when I was informed a few days later that I had passed the exam and was required to report for a physical exam as the next stage in the process. I was surprised to learn that only twelve of us had passed the written exam out of the 75 present that day. Subsequently, six of us passed the physical and were accepted for aviation cadet training. On June 17th, I was sworn into the army enlisted reserve corps to await call-up for aviation cadet training, just 13 days before I had to register for the draft. (This was to have interesting repercussions for me in 1953, as I will describe later.) After being sworn in, we were told to go home and wait for our orders, which would come in 60 to 90 days.

This was somewhat of a blow, since I had quit my job, said my goodbyes, and was prepared to go off to the war! Sheepishly, I returned home with the news that I would still be around for a while. While my parents accepted this as good news, I'm not sure anyone else did, but there I was. The months passed without any further word; I still hadn't heard anything by September. I learned that others in my status had requested active duty, were taken into the army, and were serving at Fort Sheridan, an army base just north of Chicago. Although I had gone back to my job as a lab analyst at the Hammond Metals Refining Plant in Hammond, Indiana, I didn't want to wait any longer for call-up. I asked for active duty and, on November 23rd, 1942, was sent to Fort Sheridan for induction. In the interest of providing a flavor of the times, I quote from the diary that I started to keep when I first entered the service:

"Monday, November 23, 1942.

Left on 12 o'clock train for Fort Sheridan. When I got there, I was given a physical and assigned to barracks (E606). (Note: this was in the Recruit Reception Center or RRC, a jumble of temporary buildings hastily constructed to process the many thousands of recruits pouring through there.) Next morning went to warehouse and got uniforms and equipment. In the afternoon went through testing, insurance, and classification. Didn't get back to barracks until 8 and had to double time to catch up to group leaving to hear the Articles of War. Had just gotten my shots previously. One guy on each arm!! Didn't get back from Articles until 11.

Wed. 25th : Didn't do much. Mailed home clothes, caught up on sleep, and finished processing. Arms sore from shots.

Thur. Thanksgiving: It's cold out today. The assistant barracks leader seemed determined to get us to drill but we got out of it. Went to church with a guy who was kicked out of the Marines for bad conduct. Seems to have changed some. We both enjoyed the service. Sure had a good Thanksgiving dinner. My first away from home.

Friday: Drilled 2 hours this morning and is it cold out! Was assigned to guard duty tonight and was learning General Orders when Asst. Barracks Leader Bill Henderson informed me to stand by for 'shipping out'; at last we're leaving the RRC.

Left early Saturday morning in trucks. Got to 1607th during inspection and was rather impressed by large barracks and all. Soon learned!!"

On the whole, I had a rugged but pleasant stay at the Fort. When I went up there, I had visions of driving a truck or something like that. Instead we had basic infantry training. We were issued 12-gauge shotguns, bayonets, packs, cartridge belts, mess-kits & canteens, helmets, and those good old overshoes.

On Monday morning, we were gently awakened by a sweet little old sergeant (he was probably in his 30s, but to us teenagers, he was old), who obviously hated potential aviation cadets more than any other form of life, shouting obscenities that even now I hesitate to put into print. The essence of it was that after breakfast we were to fall out with rifles, galoshes, and full field packs for a ten mile hike in the wet, slushy snow. We had to borrow Springfield rifles for these hikes for full effect. My heart sank; I had applied for aviation cadet training specifically in order to avoid this kind of foolish machismo nonsense (as well as to learn to fly). Suffice it to say, I survived the physical indignities of prolonged close order drill (I can still hear the sergeant shouting, "Hornbeck, get your head up! You didn't lose anything out here!"; "but Sarge, I'm just trying to keep from stepping on the heels of the guy ahead of me"); cleanup crew "All I want to see are assholes and elbows!"; bayonet drill "Get him in the gut, twist the bayonet, and then pull it out"; and finally, pulling targets for the MPs."

The contingent of MPs (military police) had regular target practice on the rifle ranges. Targets were made of paper and about a yard square, mounted on a wooden frame that slid up and down in grooves on either side. Our job was to wait in the trenches below the targets (one man below each target) while the rifle bullets whizzed above our heads, hopefully hitting and going through the targets and not ricocheting off the dirt, where they could be a positive menace. After several rounds had been fired and the firing stopped, we would pull the targets down, note the locations of each hit, cover the holes with appropriate patches (white patches on white parts of the target, black on the black portions), push the targets back up, then, with a small circle on the end of a pole, show the locations of the hits in the black areas by the white side of the circle and the locations of hits in the white area by the black side of the circle. I believe that we waved a red flag for the number of shots that missed the target completely, but this little detail is somewhat hazy in my memory. Anyway, it was almost as much fun as K.P., especially on those raw, windy, winter days near the shores of Lake Michigan.

The days that followed were a steady routine of calisthenics, close-order drill, hikes, marksmanship (we used .22-cal rifles on an indoor range), bayonet practice, training films, pulling targets, and guarding the rifle range. I fired for record on the .22-cal range and qualified for expert with a score of 186 out of a possible 200. I had done some shooting in the High School ROTC. Quoting again from my diary:

"Highlights were week-end passes and going home over Sat. & Sun., if we passed inspection Sat. morning. Restricted once for insufficiently shined boots after being all packed and everything. Disappointing, no end!

Spent a rather lonely Christmas, with exception of wonderful dinner, a G.I. marvel. Went to church service Xmas eve. Was glad to get home for real Xmas on Sat. & Sun. Found out date of (cadet) appointment to be Jan. 5, for Nashville.

Was home New Year's Eve to Sun. nite. Said final goodbyes in preparation for leaving Tuesday. Went on standby Monday morning just as we were preparing for long hike in the snow with full field packs.

Had to stand out in bitter cold for an hour Tue. to get paid. Left on North Shore for 8th St. Theatre in Chicago at noon with new-found pal, Howard Mariska. Tamarin, Engh, Revord also along.

Left Chicago at eight in the evening, 30 servicemen and about 500 civilians. Howie and I were appointed car commanders to maintain order.

Finally arrived at Nashville about 1600 the next day, with not a bite to eat since 1800 the nite before. After chow were assigned to barracks and Howie & I appointed barracks chief and asst. Men were promptly put on K.P. until 2200, while we cleaned up the barracks. As "old G.I.s" we gave the men a pep talk that night in preparation for cleaning up for inspection in the morning. Cleanest barracks were to leave casual and go through processing first, so we were eager and men responded fine. Passed inspection and we went through processing. (They took my mess-kit, canteen, leggings, fatigue hat, and the best item of all, my field jacket, and gave me cadet hat, oxfords, gas mask, cadet insignia, extra sun-tans, etc.) We were assigned to Sqdn. F-2 and, barracks bags over our shoulders, marched off to our new quarters. After some difficulty and much sweating, we finally got there, and disgustedly saw they were the same tar-paper, pot-belly-stoved shacks as in casual. I was destined to live a month in those bare, bleak huts, shivering in GI cots with long underwear on and 2 blankets, a quilt, and my overcoat for covering, no sheets or pillow-cases. Used a T-shirt to cover my pillow. One morning it was so cold the mop water froze on the floor as the mop was drawn across it. This, in 'sunny Tennessee'. One afternoon the thermometer read 78 degrees F., the next morning it was 17 degrees.

The next day (Jan. 7th) we started taking the classification examinations, the first being an interview with an officer to determine our A.R.M.A. (Adaptability Rating for Military Aviation). It just seemed like they asked a lot of unimportant and irrelevant questions, but it proved to be the cause for washing out several fellows. Then came a stiff and intensive physical. Passed everything O.K. except for one thing, one 'doc' seemed to think I had a heart murmur, so I had to take a recheck the next Monday. With the crazy thing I did the night before, it was no wonder! I went over to the latrine about 2100, preparing to go to bed early. There I started talking with Howie, Joe Praczer, and another fellow named Joe from New York. By the time we were through, after a lively discussion of politics (Joe wanted to be a ruthless politician), engineering (Praczer's choice), music (Howie's ambition), science (my field), and psychology, sociology, religion, motives for joining the cadets, and a thousand other things, it was 2 in the morning, so I only got in four hours sleep that night. But we sure enjoyed the little tete-a-tete.

Anyhow, I took it easy over the weekend and passed the recheck without the slightest bit of trouble. There I was, with two majors straining their eardrums, and they couldn't find anything wrong. Then I had to wait two weeks before taking my "psychs," and in the meantime, Howie & the others finished their examinations and were classified. All this time, the fellows were getting details of K.P. & guard duty right and left, but since I was appointed a cadet lieutenant (B Flight, barracks 3 & 4) I didn't get any, myself."

That was the last entry in my diary; although I saved the little book, I never did get around to putting anything more in it.

While I was waiting to get back on stream in the classification process, Howie and the others in our group received their shipping orders. **All sixty-five, (regardless of classification!), were sent off to navigator school somewhere in the East Coast Command.** If I had not been required to have a recheck, I probably would have gone off with them and become a navigator. In retrospect, the recheck was one of the luckiest things that ever happened to me.

I have not remarked much on any of the individuals I had met in this first stage of my experiences as an aviation cadet. Most of them blur into the background; I can remember a few faces but can attach no names to them, and never met any of them again. The one person I remember quite distinctly is Howie, (Howard Mariska). He was several years older than I was (upper age limit for aviation cadets was 26) and obviously had more education than I. He was a very good friend during the brief time we were together and expanded my thinking considerably. He was interested in poetry and even encouraged me to write a few things. One of the things I wrote I was called "Flight":

RP322 Lightning I (P38 trainer)

Flight

Thing of beauty!
Swimming in a shoreless ocean,
No more transfixed to this eternal globe.
Free, unbound,
Unhampered in its motion,
Steed supreme to reign 'bove land and sea.

Another one, inspired by my interest in astronomy and science fiction, was untitled:

> Huge spheres of matter revolving about gigantic suns
> intermixed with cold satellites and fiery comets,
> But still -- emptiness!
>
> The whole is made up of its parts
> And yet the whole is not here;
> A million million parts scattered throughout
> all universes and eternities,
> now present at the birth of a new star,
> now witnessing the destruction of a nebula eons away.
> All yearning, burning with a desire to become a Whole.
>
> I, alone, am I!
> But an infinitude of voices cries out
> "Are we not you?"

I don't know what became of Howard. We parted company at NAAC and went our separate ways. I tried to contact him after the war but was not able to locate him.

2

Preflight and Primary Training

On to Preflight

All of us who had been classified for pilot training were assigned to the class of 43-I. Class designators indicated the year and approximate month of graduation. On February 3rd, we received orders to be loaded on a train and shipped to the preflight school in Santa Ana, California. Four hundred pilot cadets were loaded on the train. All had been perfect physical specimens when they arrived in Nashville and now, after stays of 2 to 4 weeks at NAAC were being shipped to California. As an indication of how severe living conditions were at NAAC, about fifty cadets were taken off the train at various places for emergency medical care, most with pneumonia, severe bronchitis, or other respiratory ailments. By the time we got to Santa Ana at four o'clock one morning, after several days on the train (I don't remember how many days but it was at least four), 75 of us, including myself, went on sick call. I was immediately assigned to the hospital with a severe case of tonsillitis. After two or three weeks, I was released from the hospital and had fallen back another class. I was now in the class of 43-J. This was the group I was destined to stay with for the remainder of my cadet life.

We heard later that a Congressional investigation had been launched to look into conditions at Nashville. I don't know if anything ever came of it, but I hoped that conditions there improved for some of the later arrivals.

Here I was, at last, in preflight school and ready to begin training. Santa Ana had many thousands of cadets at various stages of preflight training. (My recollection is that there were 30,000 cadets on the base. All of the flying schools in the west coast training command received students from there.) The Army pilot program consisted of four phases, each lasting approximately two and a half months: preflight, primary flying school, basic flying school, and advanced flying school. While in basic, the decision was made as to the type of advanced training to be received, i.e., single- or twin-engine fighter, twin- or multi-engine bomber, etc. This choice dictated which type of advanced flying school you would be sent to.

In preflight school, we studied typical ground school subjects such as theory of flight, navigation, meteorology, aircraft engines, etc., with some specific military subjects thrown in: aircraft and ship identification, Morse code, military organization and command structure, weapons, etc. Of course, there was always close order drill, calisthenics, and similar forms of subtle torture, but I managed to tough it out. I have to admit that when we returned to the barracks after a particularly long hike or exhausting period of calisthenics, I would flop on my cot until the others had jostled their way through their showers, then take mine, and go running out the door, buttoning my shirt, falling into the rear rank as they marched off.

There were about 150 of us in Squadron 37, commanded by a Lt. Hicks, but we had our own cadet officers for day-to-day activities in the squadron. After we had been on the base for several weeks we were given 24-hour passes on Saturday afternoons to go into Los Angeles. Seven of us would pool our resources and hire a limousine for the trip into town; it was the cheapest, most accessible, and easiest way to go. I got in with a group of young people at the Covenant Church and usually stayed with one of the church families. Getting back to camp was usually done by hitchhiking; there was no problem getting rides if you were in uniform. We had to be back for the big parade at 3 o'clock every Sunday afternoon. Many of the guys, especially the older ones, were really hung over and couldn't take standing in the hot sun on parade. They would drop like flies, and stretcher bearers were busy keeping the parade ground clear of fallen bodies. They always said "Never again," but the same bunch would be dropping again the next Sunday.

Not much of consequence occurred in preflight, but one thing was noteworthy. We had a squadron bugler by the name of George Boldi. He would play "Taps" for us on his trumpet every night and afterward would play a sweet melody or a haunting refrain. He was really good and we enjoyed it very much. One thing he played was called "Gloomy Sunday" and it was truly a haunting refrain, beautiful but melancholic.

Recently, a good friend of my wife's, someone we had known for many years here in Livermore, California, mentioned that her family name was Boldi. I knew that some members of her family were quite musical and so I asked if she had a relative named George who played the trumpet. She looked at me in amazement and replied that yes, she had a cousin by that name, who had been in the Air Force and was about my age. It was indeed the same George Boldi, but unfortunately he had died just a few months before. He and his wife had actually been to Livermore several times on visits, but we hadn't known about each other. He was in the same squadron with me in primary flying school, but we went separate ways for basic flying school and lost touch.

The great day finally came when we had done our last Sunday afternoon parade and were off to the next stage: primary flying school. We were sent to a civilian flying school called "Mira Loma Flight Academy" near Oxnard, in the beautiful Santa Barbara valley. We were to train in Stearman PT13s, a neat little biplane with a 225-hp radial engine. The excitement and sense of anticipation was almost unbearable -- we were actually going to fly!

Stearman PT13 Primary Trainer

Mira Loma Flight Academy

On April 17, 1943, about two hundred hopefuls arrived at Mira Loma and were assigned in groups of fifty to Squadrons 3, 4, 7, and 8. Although this was a civilian school, military discipline and protocol was still observed. For example, in order to have the marching formations look as good as possible, all 200 of us were lined up according to height. The first fifty (tallest) were assigned to Squadron 3, the next fifty to Squadron 4, etc. Being in the shortest group, I ended up in Squadron 8. As in the other flight schools we were to attend, the other four squadrons (1, 2, 5, & 6) consisted of the cadets in the class ahead of us, 43-I, who were now the upperclassmen. Naturally, as lower class men we were subjected to a great deal of hazing by them. It was all part of the scene and most of it was in a spirit of fun, although at times it could be very frustrating. I'll never forget the time we were standing inspection (we had to stand at attention in front of our bunks) and these two upper class cadet officers came in to give us a rough time. One of them stood directly in front of me, looked me in the eye, and shouted out "Is damn Yankee one word or two?" He was obviously a "gentleman" of the Old South. I was so freaked out I don't know what I answered, but it must have been satisfactory because he didn't have me on the floor doing pushups (a favorite form of amusement for upperclassmen).

Living conditions were quite decent -- no more army-type barracks or dormitories. We were assigned to small huts, four to a hut, but open inside, i.e., no individual rooms, just four bunks and four desks, and a separate lavatory. One of my roommates was our cadet wing adjutant, Jimmy House. (I haven't been able to remember who the other two were.) Jimmy was a splendid fellow, capable, good-natured, an excellent horseman, and a natural pilot. Among those in our squadron who had never flown before, he was the first to solo. Average number of hours of flight instruction before soloing was about eight; he did it in five and a half. (It took me the full eight.) Jimmy's sister was married to the movie actor Andy Devine and one day Andy came to the hut to take him out for a visit. It was the first time I had met a movie star and was impressed, especially since I had always enjoyed him in his pictures.

We were divided into groups of five for flight instruction. My instructor was a middle-aged civilian pilot by the name of Brandt. He had been a civilian pilot and an instructor for many years and really knew how to handle that Stearman. From his years of flying in an open cockpit plane, his face was tanned and leathery, but around the edges of his face, the skin that was covered by his flying helmet was as soft and pink as a baby's. On my first flight with him, he took off, gained a couple of thousand feet of altitude, and proceeded to show me all the things the plane could do. Then he had me take the controls. I did all those things student pilots do when first given the controls of an airplane, that must, at times, drive instructors to exasperation. However, he was both firm and patient, and soon had me more relaxed and doing rather well. Then he hit me with a bombshell. Over the Gosport tubes he ordered, "O.K., take me back to the field." I looked wildly about; I hadn't the slightest idea which direction the field was in, and he knew it! After a good chewing out, he took the controls and headed for the field. Never again did I fail to keep track of the direction to the field. (The Gosport tubes were hollow tubes going from a small funnel in the front cockpit to the plug-ins on the student's helmet. It was the only way you could hear the instructor over the engine's roar. There was no way for the student to talk back to the instructor unless you really shouted.

One of the other students in our group of five, surprisingly, was a fellow from Chicago by the name of Don Kelly. He lived just a block down the street from me on Maryland Avenue. I didn't know him because he was a few years older than I was, but I did know and had gone to school with his younger brother, Marvin. It seemed almost miraculous that we had lived so close and were now two thousand miles from home and assigned to the same instructor in flight school. We had arrived there by quite different routes, as well. Being older, he had been drafted into the army. Being a real operator, he had worked himself into the position of being an armorer in a searchlight battalion. He claimed they had one or two .30-cal machine guns to be taken care of, but if I know Kelly, they probably didn't have any. They had completed their training and Kelly could see the handwriting on the wall: they would soon be shipped overseas. That was something he wasn't the slightest bit interested in and so he did the most desperate thing he could and applied for flight school. He was accepted, pulled out of the battalion, and sent to cadet school. He was with me for the rest of my training and got his wings and commission. However, at that point he was on the brink of possibly going into combat and he pulled another maneuver, of which more, later. He was a real con artist and a great card player; his ambition was to open a small card room on the South Side of Chicago after the war. He would have been quite successful. I'll say this for him: he played honestly and adroitly, he didn't cheat, and he never gambled with us, or any of the other cadets. However, he liked nothing better than cleaning out a bunch of GIs or Navy gobs. Mostly, we played "Hearts" for fun and sometimes Kelly would join in on the game. He usually won; after each hand he could tell us the cards each person had held and how they had been played, and how we could have beaten him if we had paid better attention!

For all that, he was not a great student and usually sat next to me when we had examinations in ground school. Although I was a good student, I was frequently tired from the heavy schedule we had, especially in basic when we started night flying. Occasionally I would doze off during an exam and he would nudge me and whisper "Wake up, Robert F., I need the answer to the next question!"

In spite of the differences between us, we became good friends and had good times together.

But back to the flying! I loved it, even more than I thought I would. In spite of a few queasy moments on that first flight, especially after Mr. Brandt's demonstration of three-turn tailspins and inverted flight, I never experienced air sickness in any form, and for that was thankful. Some of the guys did, but were able to overcome it. Others were not able to do so and eventually quit or were washed out.

The great day came when the instructor got out of the plane and told me to take it up myself. Without an instructor in it, that front cockpit became a huge, gaping hole -- a vivid reminder that you were on your own. Full of anticipation and excitement, I made my takeoff, climbed to altitude, and followed the traffic pattern around, turning onto the downwind leg, the base leg, and then the final approach. Although excited, I wasn't fearful and was determined to make a good landing. As I came in, I wasn't satisfied with the final approach and gave it the gun to go around. On the second approach, I again was dissatisfied and gave it the gun a second time. About this time my instructor was chewing his nails, thinking that I was afraid to land (it sometimes happens to students on their solo flights). Finally, on the third approach I decided to take her all the way in and made a satisfactory, if not spectacular, landing. After I had taxied in and got out of the plane he said, "I thought we were going to have to shoot you down!"

When we got back from the flight line that afternoon, I, and several others who had soloed that day, were ceremoniously thrown into the swimming pool. From that time on, I proudly wore the white scarf (the badge of having soloed) when in my flying togs.

After Soloing

It wasn't too long before we had to face that terrible ordeal, the twenty-hour check ride. An instructor known as "Laughing Boy" McLean, also "Screaming McLean," gave the check rides in our squadron. No one in the history of man had known him to so much as crack a smile. Although we didn't realize it at the time, he performed an important function and in the long run made us better pilots. There is nothing more dangerous in the sky than a fledgling pilot who is a "hot shot" and thinks he is God's gift to the world of aviation. It was the check pilot's responsibility to disabuse him of that notion and bring him back to reality. And McLean was a master at it!

After flubbing my way through the routine, stall and spin recovery maneuvers, etc., he ordered me to shoot some landings at our auxiliary airfield. As I approached the field, I carefully noted the flight pattern and the direction of landing as indicated by the large "tee," which was rotated manually in accordance with the wind direction. With great care I entered the traffic pattern on the downwind leg, turned onto the base leg, and then onto the final approach. Suddenly, I heard the voice of Screaming McLean blasting through on the Gosport tubes, "Look at that silly sonovabitch down there waving the red flag." I looked carefully and indeed, there was a silly sonovabitch down there waving a red flag -- at me! The traffic pattern had been reversed and the tee turned around since I approached the field and I was now about to land in the face of several planes taking off. McLean jerked the controls away from me and silently took us back and landed at the main field. I figured this was it...this is how it feels to be washed out...never to fly again except possibly as a gunner on an air crew...Oh the ignominy of it all!

When we got out of the airplane, my worst fears were confirmed.

McLean, at maximum volume, informed me that I was, beyond doubt, the poorest excuse for an aviation cadet he had ever had the misfortune to give a check ride to. He was unable to understand how I had gotten this far in the program but could see that I'd never make it any farther. He then proceeded to lambaste me for virtually every move I had made on the check ride, thus buttressing his argument that I had absolutely no redeeming qualities for military aviation. By the time I was dismissed, I had been reduced to a mass of jelly, and I returned to my instructor devoid of all hope or purpose. He, however, allowed as how I might do better with a few more hours of instruction and might pass the next time. And so I did. Eventually, of course, I learned that "Screaming McLean" launched virtually the same diatribe against every cadet on his first check ride. It kept them humble.

Two things were drilled into our skulls before we had even started flying: first, that every other plane in the sky with us had but one purpose, to head directly for us with a deliberate goal of a head-on crash and that you had better not relax your constant vigilance for even a moment. (As they said, keep your head on a swivel!) The second thing was that there are old pilots and there are bold pilots but there no old, bold pilots. That, in essence, we were there not only to learn to fly, but to survive.

Among the things we learned in primary were two maneuvers called crossroad eights and pylon eights. They were exercises to teach you how to follow a pattern on the ground while compensating for wind drift. A crossroad eight was performed by picking a right-angle cross road and executing an eight-shaped figure which used the center of the intersection as the center of the eight, while keeping lined up with the roads in each direction. It was a simple maneuver and one soon learned to crab into the wind so that you tracked the roads on the ground.

The pylon eight was more difficult. For this maneuver, one had to be at an altitude above the ground consistent with one's airspeed and rate of turn to make it work. This altitude was 540 feet for the PT13 at cruising speed and in a standard 30-degree bank turn. Our minimum allowed flying altitude was 500 feet, so it was executable within our minimums. The maneuver was accomplished by picking two similar, isolated objects on the ground a given distance apart. They could be poles, barns, whatever was convenient. One then flew an eight-shaped figure with the "pylons" in the centers of the lobes of the eights. You would find that on the upwind side of the pylon you had to lessen your angle of bank to keep from drifting into the pylon, while on the downwind side you had to steepen your angle of bank to keep from drifting away from it. Properly executed, it was a smooth, coordinated maneuver, with your wingtip pointed directly at the appropriate pylon throughout the turn.

All this is by way of introduction to two interesting experiences I had involving these maneuvers. The first time I tried pylon eights while solo, I had gone further up the valley than usual to avoid all of the traffic nearer to the airfield. Although I tried my best, I just couldn't make the pylon eights work out right; soon my hour was up and I had to return to the field. After I landed and got out of the plane, I received an order to report immediately to the Squadron Commander's office. On arriving there, I was met by the C.O. and another flight instructor, who vociferously accused me of "buzzing" the farms up the valley (a wash-out offense, I might add). At that point in my flying career I had no intention of putting myself into such jeopardy and immediately denied it. He asserted that he himself had seen me flying at 200-300 feet. I replied that couldn't have been me because I had been practicing pylon eights and had carefully kept my altitude at 540 feet but that I hadn't been able to get them to work right. About this time, the C.O. smiled and asked me if that was what my altimeter had read. I replied that it had. He then proceeded to give me a lecture about the fact that the altimeter gave the altitude above sea level and that the valley floor was 200-300 feet above sea level at that point. (Our home field was almost at sea level so the altimeter was set to zero before we took off). He also pointed out, in no uncertain terms, that I should have known better and that I had better not forget it again...and I never did. Another lesson well learned.

The other incident occurred a week or so later. Every day we had this low stratus come in from the ocean and we would have a solid overcast with a ceiling of about 800 feet all day long. The ceiling was too low to do any aerobatics, but we had to get our flying time in or the class would fall behind, so every day it was crossroad eights and pylon eights. This culminated in a once in a lifetime experience for me that was so vivid that I celebrated it in 1967 with a poem called "Local Flying Only."

Local Flying Only

"Ceiling eight hundred feet, sky overcast, light winds
from the west southwest.
Solo students released for local flying only."

So had it been this past grey week,
Downhearted we trudged to our waiting craft,
Parachutes slung over shoulders with careful abandon,
White scarves flicking in the light but chilling breeze.

Fledgling pilots we, newly soloed, aching to measure
our newfound wings
Against the heights of the vast blue sky,
Yet doomed to spend another day beneath the blanket
valley wide,
So thick, so impenetrable.

Over and over again, guiding our machines in crossroad
eights and pylon eights,
Wing high on the downwind side, now low on the upwind,
Around, around, would the sky never open and cut from us
the chains of earth so near below...

Suddenly a splash of light on a hill close by,
A patch of blue appears above me.
With a hasty, but guilty, look about
(Having already committed the misdeed in my mind)
I shove the throttle forward, the throbbing craft leaps
to its challenge.
Up, up in a dizzying spiral until, behold
The sun, a brilliant blazing orb in a sea of crystal blue,
The sky unblemished above,
A smooth white blanket beneath,
Punctuated here and there by the tips of dark, sullen hilltops,
Solitary, grim sentinels of the earth that would have me back,
however reluctantly.

But not yet, earth -- I must stretch these wings a moment more
-- what's this?
A craft below me following silently, relentlessly,
It's but the shadow of my own, circled with a fragile halo,
Such wonders to be discovered -- please mother...God...
can't I stay out a little longer?

My escape hatch is disappearing, the trapdoor to the dull, dark cellar is closing
And there is no other.
Quickly, throttle back, tight spiral downward
And I am again in the thin layer below.
The leaden clouds above, the unforgiving earth beneath, jealous of my moment of freedom,
A moment of vision and beauty locked in my heart,
Occasionally to be taken down from the shelf and stroked like a soft, furry animal
On dark and gloomy days to come.

Another flying experience that I recall from primary is a bit more mundane -- it has to do with passing a check ride on landing short over a fence. A rope was stretched across the runway at a height of 6 or 8 feet and we were to come in slow, with a slight amount of power. On crossing over the rope, you were supposed to chop the throttle and land as short as possible on the other side of the rope. (The check pilot was standing at the end of the runway watching the whole procedure). I came dragging in on low power, barely maintaining flying speed. As I came up to the end of the runway, the plane began to sink and I knew I couldn't make it over the rope! The very worst thing one could do in this maneuver was to fly into the rope and cut it or become entangled in it -- that would quickly establish one's reputation as the poorest pilot in the squadron. In desperation, I eased in a little throttle, popped the stick forward, bounced the wheels over the rope, and, easing off on the throttle made a nice three-point landing just barely past the rope. Although it didn't qualify as passing the test, it was hailed as an imaginative solution to the position I had put myself in, and I was given another crack at it.

The Stearman was an excellent flying machine but it had real limitations on the ground. It had a very narrow landing gear; the narrow gear, combined with the high center of gravity of a biplane, meant that it could easily veer to one side in a landing, especially in a crosswind. Under these circumstances, one of two conditions could ensue. In trying to keep the plane tracking a straight line down the runway, it could tip to the side until the end of the lower wing dragged along the ground (a "wing-drag"). On the other hand, it could completely get away from you and spin around in a "ground loop," also dragging the lower wingtip. If either of these happened, the tip of the wing would probably be damaged and would have to be repaired. One of the absolute no-no's was to do anything that would require repairs on the plane and therefore keep it out of operation, since there was so much emphasis on keeping everything flying to maximize the number of flying hours attainable. Any such accident resulted in an immediate check ride by one of the top check pilots, one of the things most feared by student pilots, since it could lead to the dreaded "w" word -- washout!

One day, landing in a crosswind, the plane started veering and I took immediate corrective action, but it didn't seem to be sufficient. As I was going down the runway with the wingtip just skirting the ground, I had this intense and dramatic vision of a newspaper headline, proclaiming in very large type, "HORNBECK DRAGS WINGTIP - DAMAGES PLANE!" It was most unsettling, especially since I thought I could see clouds of dust being kicked up by the wingtip. I kept the plane under control and taxied back to the ramp. A member of the ground crew had watched the entire maneuver and met me as I taxied in. Walking alongside the plane, he surreptitiously felt the underside of the wingtip, smiled, and passed me a sign that it was undamaged. It seems like a trivial event now, but at the time it seemed I had the weight of the world on my back until I got the reassuring sign.

For me, primary was absolutely an incredible experience, probably one of the happiest periods in my life. It was a busy and challenging time, taken up almost completely with learning to fly and learning all of the attendant subjects in ground school. Basic and advanced flying schools were also fun, and included some of the more specialized aspects of military flying: instrument training, navigation, formation flight, aerial gunnery, night flying, etc.

As one would expect, some of the guys couldn't hack it in primary. We had our share of students who couldn't get rid of motion sickness, others who froze on the controls until the instructor had to force the stick away, and others who just plain didn't want to stay with it for any number of reasons. Those of us who made it through primary became committed pilots, loving the experience and looking forward to any additional challenges it might bring. Thus, World War II enabled me to attain my fondest goal, learning to fly.

3

Basic flying school

Polaris Flight Academy

Mira Loma was owned and operated by a man by the name of Moseley. He also owned and operated a basic flying school called Polaris Flight Academy out in the Mojave desert near Lancaster, California. Almost all of the basic flying schools were run by the army; as far as I know, Polaris was the only civilian basic flying school in the program. One fine day in June 1943 we had completed our 65 hours of flight training in the PT13 at Mira Loma and were shipped off to Polaris to begin basic.

Living conditions were very much like they were at Mira Loma. Although administrative and personnel functions were the province of army personnel stationed at the school, the flight instructors were civilians. I can recall quite clearly the face of the instructor I had and many of his mannerisms, but have been unable to recall his name. He was an older pilot, with graying hair and a gray moustache, but an excellent instructor and demanding taskmaster. Unfortunately, I do not have a class book from basic (as I do from primary and advanced training) -- I might have had one at one time, but if so, it seems to have been lost over the years.

We flew the BT13, affectionately known as the "Vultee Vibrator." It had a 450-hp radial engine, a two-speed, variable pitch propeller, and was a low-wing, all-metal monoplane with manually operated wing flaps for landing and take off. It also had a plexiglass canopy, two-way radios, an interphone for communication between the front and rear seats, instruments suitable for instrument flying, and selectable gas tanks. It seemed huge, powerful, and complex to us.

After the usual transition training (learning how to take off, land,

and just generally fly the plane), we got into the more specialized areas of military flying, all of which I enjoyed tremendously. There was formation flying (we did take-offs in formation but not landings), navigation, instrument training, learning to fly the "beam" (the radio range stations), and night flying. I especially enjoyed night flying and became quite interested in night fighters. I wanted to fly the Northrop P61, the "Black Widow," and so, when the time came to apply for advanced flying school, I requested night fighters (but I am getting ahead of my story).

Instructor & student in BT13

Two particular flying incidents from basic stand out in my memory. The first occurred while I was learning to fly at night, the second was related to instrument training. As I mentioned, the BT13 had selectable fuel tanks. There was one in the wing on each side of the plane and by looking down at the floor, the fuel gauges could be seen on each side of the cockpit. They were illuminated at night and could be seen both by the instructor in the rear seat and the student in the front seat. Standard procedure before take-off was to switch the selector valve to the tank with the most fuel in it. The tank selector valve was located on the lower left corner of the instrument panel and had three positions, left, right, and off. A rod extended from the center of the selector valve handle along the side of the cockpit terminating in a similar valve handle on the instructor's panel in the rear cockpit. There was a thickened portion of the rod that the student could grasp with his left hand to rotate the valve without having to reach forward to turn the valve handle itself. Since the position indicator on the valve handle was not lighted, we were told that at night we were always to reach forward and turn the valve handle so that we could feel which position it was in. This was really good advice (but not always recognized as so by students).

I was shooting night landings with my instructor at an auxiliary field on Rosamund Dry Lake out in the desert. The "field" consisted of runways painted on the hard, dry lake bed, which was flat and packed hard in all directions. I had made one landing and was taxiing around to take off for another trip around the flight pattern for another landing. I checked the fuel gauges and saw that the right tank was fuller than the left one, which I had been using. Reaching up with my left hand, I rotated the rod one position clockwise, putting the selector on the right tank. I went through the runup procedure, lined up with the runway, and proceeded to take off. I had barely gotten into the air, when a bright, white light lit up the instrument panel and blinded me. Shortly thereafter, the engine quit and I had to "feel" the plane down, not being able to see out into the darkness with that bright light in my face. With a couple of miles of hard, flat surface ahead of me, this was no big problem, and I soon brought the plane to a stop. Then I figured out what had happened. Unknown to me, the instructor had already switched the gas selector valve to the right tank. When I reached up to rotate the rod, I had switched the gas off, and didn't realize it because I had not leaned forward and grasped the valve handle itself. This is not a very wise thing to do just before takeoff! The carburetor had enough fuel in it to get us into the air, then ran out. The bright light in my face was the fuel pressure warning light, which had lost its red cover. By this time, however, my face was red enough to make up for it. I got a royal chewing out because I had not followed correct procedure, and deserved it. I never did know whether the instructor had switched the tank absent-mindedly without telling me or had done it deliberately to test my reaction. I suspect the latter. He probably had not realized the red cover was missing on the warning light and the peril we would have been in if I had stalled out or flubbed up the landing. A similar incident at our main field would have been fatal. There were power lines at the end of the runway that would have clobbered us. Needless to say, I never again switched tanks at night without leaning forward to grasp the selector valve handle. As all pilots know, not only are there no old bold pilots, there are no old unlucky ones.

The other incident occurred while I was flying as "safety pilot" on an instrument training flight. For instrument practice, two students would be assigned an "instrument" plane for a two-hour period. These were special planes with good gyro horizons (also known as flight indicators) and were never allowed to be used for acrobatics. One student, in the front seat, would take off and land the plane. The other student, in the rear seat, had a canvas hood that he could pull over him to keep him from seeing out of the plane. Once up to altitude, he would pull the cover in place and proceed to fly the plane on instruments, while the student in front kept scanning the sky for other planes.

One day I was acting as safety pilot while my friend Hutchison was "under the hood." After he had finished his practice, I took over the controls and told him to come out from under the hood, since I was in a hurry to get back. He said "Like this?" and popped the stick forward a bit. Responding, I said "No, like this!" and shoved the stick forward hard. I heard a noise in the cockpit behind me and was astonished and chagrined to see that he had been hurled out of his seat and his head had gone through the plexiglass canopy. He had been flying the plane with his seatbelt unfastened! I resumed level flight and was relieved to find that he had not been injured, but had lost his headphones in the slipstream. Sheepishly, I flew back to the main field and landed. Seeing us taxiing in with a big hole in the canopy, the crew chief was more than slightly upset. In very short order, we were standing before the Squadron C.O. and accused of doing acrobatics in an instrument ship. (A washout offense -- they took these things rather seriously.) Once again, I had visions of my aviation career going down the tubes...but we finally managed to convince him that it had occurred as I have described. This was not exactly a small victory, more like a less disastrous defeat. Neither of us had to take a pre-washout check ride, but did get some dramatic lessons in chewing out from the C.O. and later, our instructor. We both had committed grievous errors -- myself in executing a violent maneuver in an instrument ship and my friend in flying without his seatbelt on. We had drilled into us from the first moment that we took to the air that a student never -- but never -- unfastened his seat belt in the air. I never had done so and hadn't for a moment suspected that my friend had.

This brings to mind an incident that we had heard about involving a student in primary flight training in another training command. It seems that he had forgotten to fasten his seatbelt and his instructor was demonstrating a loop. When the plane became inverted at the top of the loop, he fell out of it. The plane came around, completed the loop and he fell onto the rear of the fuselage, clutching madly to hang on while the instructor flew back to the field and landed. This story was written up in the newspaper but I always had some doubts about whether or not it actually had occurred. Years later, I was telling my wife about it and she told me that the student in the incident came from the area around New Troy, Michigan, where she had lived and gone to high school, and that the incident was well known in the area at the time.

One other incident from basic comes to mind. One day we were heading over to the flight line and were astonished to see a parachute blossom out and come floating down not far from the field. I had mentioned earlier that the flight instructors were all civilians. It turned out that this one young flight instructor had always wanted to make a parachute jump and had received notice that he was being drafted into the army. So, he took his best student up for a dual flight, told him to take the plane back to the field, and bailed out! That man was a hero to us students for weeks after; it was a terrifically cool thing to do.

Many of us wanted to make a parachute jump and tried to get permission to make practice jumps. We were always told that there was no such thing as a practice jump; the first time you did it, it was a real one! In reality, the service couldn't afford to let cadets make "practice" jumps. Statistically, a small, but not insignificant number, would be injured and a smaller number killed (considering the state of the art of parachute jumping at the time). I guess paratroopers were more expendable than pilots, but then parachute jumping was their business and so they had to do it.

We had eighty hours of flying in basic and then went on to

advanced flight school. All of us who had applied for night fighters, along with those who had applied for twin-engine fighters, were sent to the P38 school at Williams Field near Chandler, Arizona, a few miles south of Phoenix. It was a happy group of cadets that went off to advanced training in that shipment.

Northrop P61 Black Widow

This is the plane I had set my sights on: the Northrop P61 "Black Widow" night fighter.

It was the first U.S. plane specifically designed to be a night fighter and was powered by two 2250-hp Pratt and Whitney radial engines. Although big (wingspan 66 feet) and heavy (32,000 lb loaded), it was maneuverable and powerful. It would have been exciting to fly and would have presented a real challenge.

4

Advanced Flying School

Williams Field, Arizona

Back in the army again! On arriving at Williams Field, we were immediately struck with the feeling of being back on an army base again, although it was a very nice base compared to Nashville and Santa Ana. Fifty-five of us were designated for night fighter training and assigned to Squadron 4. The remainder of the cadets in our class, destined for the regular twin-engine fighter program, were assigned to the other five squadrons.

We flew three excellent advanced trainers: the Curtis AT9 (also known as the Curtis "Rock") for transition to twin-engine flight, the single-engine AT6 (Texan) built by North American for aerial and ground gunnery, and a trainer version of the Lockheed P38, designated the RP322. The P322s were actually built for the British, and had fuel gauges calibrated in Imperial gallons (slightly larger than a U.S. gallon). One important difference was that the British ordered Lightnings without the high-speed turbo superchargers used on the U.S. models, partly because the U.S. didn't have enough units for its own use and partly because RAF ground crews didn't have the experience to maintain the machinery. In consequence, the training planes could not pull as much manifold pressure at high altitude as the U.S. operational P38s, but at the lower altitudes used in our training program, they were more than adequate.

The AT9 was a neat little twin-engine trainer. It had two 450-hp Lycoming radial engines; (the BT13 had the 450-hp "Wasp Junior".) It had a very short nose, about even with the tips of the propeller spinners (like the British Beaufighter), and two side-by-side seats for the pilot and copilot, but no room for anyone else to fly in the plane. It had constant-speed propellers, hydraulically operated wing flaps and retractable landing gear. However, hydraulic pressure was not available until you pushed down a control called the "power button," which then supplied hydraulic pressure to the system. It had conventional gear and a tail wheel lock. The tail wheel was freely rotating for easy turning on the ground but had to be locked for take-off and landing. The AT9 was unique at the time because it was the only plane in the AAF that had metal control surfaces (ailerons, elevators, and flaps). Even the combat aircraft had fabric covered control surfaces.

Flying a twin-engine airplane is quite different from flying a single-engine plane. You have better control on the ground in a twin, since you can turn the plane using engine power and don't have to rely entirely on a steerable tail wheel and brakes. Emergency procedures are considerably different and these must be drummed in until they become second nature. In a single-engine plane, if the engine quits at low altitude you have no choice but to figure out very quickly the easiest and safest place to land. In a twin, you have to figure out very quickly whether or not you can control the plane and keep flying on one engine, and then take prompt action. If your speed is too low, (below what is called the safe single-engine airspeed), you must cut the power off on both engines and belly in. If your speed is greater than that, you can increase power on the good engine (if you are not already at maximum), shut down operation of the bad engine, feather the prop (if you have full-feathering props), and keep on flying. A propeller that is feathered has the blades turned until they are lined up in the slipstream. At that point, the propeller stops turning and the engine stops. One of the great bugaboos in twin-engine flying is to have one engine fail and, in the excitement, feather the prop on the good engine. Needless to say, a great deal of the training was devoted to emergency single-engine procedure.

Our first task was to "transition" to the AT9, learning all of the aircraft systems, emergency procedures, take-offs, landings, formation flying, and finally night flying. Since we were in the night fighter program, we did more night flying than the other squadrons and also had more instrument training.

Curtis AT9s in Formation

The AT9 was a "hot" little airplane; we came in on the final approach at 110 mph and everyone swore that it stalled out and quit flying at 108. A full flap power-off landing was a wonder to behold. It was like coming in power off on a dive bombing run and leveling out just before you hit the ground. Most of our landings were with partial flaps, so that you could come in at a reasonable angle and with a little power on until ready to touch down.

One of the experiences I remember well was a large formation flight we were practicing to prepare for a graduation exercise. We had 60 AT9s in formation with four rows of 15 planes each (5 three-plane elements). We were on a wide sweep through the valley, getting everyone properly in place, and suddenly a PT13 appeared from above directly in front of us in a practice tail spin. The last thing one does before executing a practice tail spin is to make a 360-degree turn to ensure that there are no planes below you. Somehow this student failed to see 60 AT9s in formation, and spun right into us. He must have seen us at about the same time that we saw him as his plane visibly jerked when he attempted to recover from the spin. I was flying the plane on the extreme left edge of the front row and threw the plane into a violent steep bank to the left. As you can well believe, there were AT9s all over that sky, but nobody hit anyone else and, after much confusion in the traffic pattern, we all got safely down. I imagine the student in the PT13 had to change his underwear when he got back to his field. I don't know what the final consequences of the event were, but I know the Director of Training at Williams Field had a few words for the Director of Training at the primary school up the valley.

In spite of the debacle, we had a very successful mass flight on graduation day (for the upper class). I flew in the same position and had the responsibility of being the first to peel off and set the traffic pattern for all of the others as we came in to land. It was a great show with a happy end.

Before leaving the AT9, I have to relate an incident that we all heard over the radio while involved in local flying. I have mentioned the tail wheel lock that was on for take-offs and landings. After landing and before turning off the end of the runway, it was the responsibility of the copilot, at the direction of the pilot, to unlock the tail wheel. One day two students were flying together and, shortly after the plane landed, the copilot was heard calling the control tower in an excited voice. It seems he had pulled up the landing gear selector valve instead of the tail wheel lock and didn't know what to do next. Nothing could happen until hydraulic power was supplied to the system. Even then, there were presumably locks that prevented the wheels from coming up as long as the weight of the plane was on them. Nevertheless, some wise guy picked up his microphone and, before the control tower could respond, shouted "Hit the power button!" Apparently the plane had not settled completely and the full weight was not on the gear (maybe the student pilot was trying to take off again) but when the copilot hit the power button, the gear retracted, the plane settled to the runway, and both props bit the dust. Each of us in the air winced as we could almost hear the props digging into the asphalt. There was an investigation to try to find the student who had given the spurious radio transmission, but I don't think anything came of it.

I have mentioned instrument training several times but have not described the craft in which we did a lot of instrument flying, both in basic and advanced (and ever thereafter). It has been described as a heavier-than-air fixed base aerial vehicle, also known as the Link trainer. It was the forerunner of all the incredible flight simulators they have today. It was mounted so that it could rotate on its base and bank to left or right to simulate turns. Sitting inside, with the top down, was like sitting in the cockpit of a plane, with all the same controls, instruments, radio accessories, etc. that you would have in a plane. It was connected to a little gadget that traced out a flight path on the instructor's table and accurately recorded your position and altitude in accord with ground speed and heading as you flew the course (or sometimes crashed into the side of a mountain).

The Link trainer was quite valuable for learning how to orient yourself using a radio range station, to fly the "beam," and to use proper procedures when approaching an airport under instrument conditions. It also helped one to learn to fly only by the instruments and not the "seat of the pants." It was really a valuable training aid in WWII.

For gunnery we were sent to the gunnery school at Ajo, near the Mexican border. We checked out in the AT6 Texan, a great little advanced single-engine trainer built by North American. It had a 600-hp radial engine, constant-speed prop, and retractable gear. The gunnery planes each had a .30-cal machine gun mounted on the cowl, synchronized to fire through the propeller (between the blades, of course). We did both ground and aerial gunnery. The aerial gunnery was done by firing at a target sleeve towed by another plane. Several students would make passes and fire at the same sleeve. There were wax coatings on the bullets, with different colored wax for each student. When your bullets hit the sleeve, there would be a slight, colored ring around each bullet hole, identifying the student who fired it. By taking the number of hits divided by the number of rounds fired from your plane, you were given a score. I managed to do well enough to make the lowest rating, that of marksman.

I did better on the ground gunnery (which served me well in my later combat role). However, I did manage to get into a bit of trouble. The targets stood about six feet high and were attacked in a moderately steep dive. Firing was to begin at a certain distance from the target and to end at an altitude of about 100 feet above the terrain. We were not supposed to arm and charge the machine gun until we had turned onto the target and started our dive. (They didn't want students accidentally shooting each other down in the traffic pattern). After I turned on the target run, I armed the machine gun but had trouble pulling back the manual charging handle to get the first round into the magazine, so that it would fire. I kept jiggling it with my right hand and flying with the left, trying to keep lined up with the target and maintain the proper airspeed. I finally got it charged, settled back, and started blasting away. By this time I was really close to the target and had to pull up at the last second to keep from hitting it with the airplane (a hit which would not have counted). The ground dropped away slightly behind the target so I had plenty of room to pull out - well...let's say... enough. When I landed and taxied in, there was the urgent order to report immediately to the Squadron C.O. The Range Officer was there, claiming that I was so low that he couldn't see my plane behind the target. I had to admit, that was hardly in the spirit of the 100-foot minimum, although I do believe he had exaggerated some. One of the first things we learned in the aviation cadets was that there are only three possible answers to a question from an officer, "Yes sir," "No sir," and "No excuse, sir." Somehow, they weren't the slightest bit interested in the problems I had charging the machine gun, and I was slowly and thoroughly roasted.

Finally, the great day came when we were to check out in the P38 (RP322). We had been through the ground school training on the engines, fuel system, hydraulic system, emergency systems, etc., etc. We sat in the cockpits for hours memorizing the positions of all the switches, selector valves, and gauges. We had a "piggy-back" ride in one of the planes modified to carry a passenger. The radio equipment directly behind the pilot was moved and space made available for a person to squeeze in with his head over the pilot's shoulder. Our instructor took each of us up for a demonstration flight, showing us the things that would be helpful once we got up there on our own. It was one of the most exciting moments of my life when I finally climbed into the cockpit alone, went through the start-up procedure, heard those 1425-hp in-line Allison engines rumble into life, and prepared to taxi out for take off.

After going through the run-up and pre take-off check list, I lined up on the runway, pressed down on the brake pedals, and pushed the throttles smoothly forward. In order to be sure the prop governors were functioning properly, you were supposed to hold the plane with the foot brakes until the engines reached maximum rpm, then release the brakes, and begin the take-off roll. I couldn't hold the brakes and the plane began creeping forward no matter how hard I pressed. I gave up and let her go. Acceleration was terrific and I was soon at take-off speed. Coming back on the control column, the plane eased into the air, but seemed a trifle clumsy. I reached down and raised the landing gear, adjusted my throttles and flaps, and the plane started climbing like a homesick angel. I was supposed to turn out at 1500' but was up to 6000' before I could get around to it.

In terms of handling ability, it was one of the sweetest planes I've ever flown. Since the engine and propellor on the right side rotated opposite in direction to those on the left side, there was no necessity for torque corrections or trim. It had absolutely no tendency to fall off to either side in a stall and was stable, maneuverable, and fast. I would have been happy to stay in P38s and go into combat, except that I still had my heart set on night fighters and the P61 Black Widow.

After a transition period, we had a few hours of formation flying, and then a high altitude cross-country flight. That was when I learned the insidious nature of hypoxia (insufficient oxygen at high altitude).

My first experience with hypoxia was in preflight, where we all had to pass the high altitude chamber test. In this test, eight or ten students would sit in a chamber which could be evacuated to simulate air densities at high altitude. We had been instructed in proper use of the oxygen masks that we had been given and well briefed on the effects of the test. In order to meet AAF requirements, we were required to go to a simulated altitude of 18,000 feet and remain there without oxygen masks on for ten minutes. Then, we were to put on our oxygen masks and breathe pure oxygen until we reached a simulated altitude of 42,000 feet. This is the maximum altitude at which a person can absorb enough oxygen in his blood, breathing pure oxygen, and still remain functional. To go any higher, pressurization must be used.

We were told that, as the simulated altitude rose above 18,000 feet, we could delay putting on the oxygen masks if we wished to experience for ourselves the effects of anoxia. I didn't realize it at the time, but this is not a very smart thing to do. Anytime one is experiencing anoxia, brain cells are being destroyed. But we were all young daredevils and didn't give it a second thought -- we wanted to experience it all. We each had a pad of paper and were told that after reaching a simulated 18,000 feet, we were to write our names continuously as the pressure was reduced. When we felt we needed oxygen, we were to put on our oxygen masks.

The chamber door closed and the test began. In addition to the observation windows in the chamber, we were accompanied by an instructor. On the way up to 18,000 feet, one student suffered an asthma-like attack and had to be let out through an air-lock. A small percentage of the population will react like that. I presume that he was eventually eliminated from the aviation cadet program, though I don't know for certain. We got to a simulated 18,000 feet and waited for the ten minute period, writing on the tablets as we had been instructed. Then we continued on to higher altitude. As we got higher and higher, I felt better and better and half believed I could go through the test without needing any oxygen. For some strange reason, it was more and more difficult to write my name, but that didn't seem to bother me at all. Soon my pencil was making just a scribble on the paper, but so what, I felt great! About this time, the instructor grabbed my mask, slipped it over my face, and told me to breathe deeply. I don't know what the simulated altitude was at that point, but things started clearing up and I was amazed at what I had experienced. **Not one single student** had decided he needed oxygen and voluntarily put on his own mask. This was, indeed, a dramatic illustration of the effects of oxygen deprivation.

But back to my story. I was scheduled for a high-altitude cross-country flight and assigned a buddy -- a fellow student who would be going on the same route and at the same time. We were told to do our own navigation but to try to keep the other fellow in sight. We took off in our planes and started climbing up to altitude. At 10,000 feet, I put on my oxygen mask and adjusted the regulator. It was a demand system; oxygen did not flow continuously but was supplied as you breathed in. Everything was going fine as we climbed out on course. As we got up to near our designated altitude, my friend called me on the radio and asked if there was something wrong with my plane. I responded that everything was fine. He came back and said that my plane was not level, that I was flying with one wing low. I concentrated hard on the horizon and, by golly, he was right. That explained why I was having so much trouble staying on course! Immediately, the nature of my predicament hit me and I leveled the wings, dropped the nose, and started checking my oxygen supply. It turned out that the demand regulator had not been properly set and that I wasn't getting any oxygen. After making things right, I was able to climb back on course and continue the flight. The value of the buddy system was well demonstrated. Alone in a situation like that, an inexperienced pilot could continue until he became unconscious and could come to as his plane reached a low altitude, out of control, and perhaps with insufficient room to recover from the maneuver.

Until we had arrived at advanced, we had not had any fatalities in our class among the students we had known. Many students had been eliminated (washed out) for failure to make the grade, and some had experienced minor accidents. However, we did have two classmates killed in advanced training, both of them in P38s as I recall. I knew both of them, and saw one of the accidents (described below) but don't remember the details of the other.

One of the students was coming in for a landing and had to "go around." This means: advancing the throttles to full power, retracting the landing gear, "milking up" the flaps as speed increases, and then turning in the traffic pattern to prepare for another attempt at landing. One has to be prepared to do this at any time during a landing if some other plane gets in the way or something happens on the runway that could prevent landing. The student advanced the throttles to full power but, as sometimes happens, one engine caught and the other one didn't. There he was, at low speed, with full power in one engine and none in the other, about the worst position you can be in, especially in a powerful twin-engine plane like the P38. Instead of chopping the throttle on the good engine and bellying in, as an experienced pilot would have done, he tried to hold it with aileron and rudder so he could keep on flying. The plane went into a steep, almost vertical bank, turned away from the runway, and the wingtip hit a low embankment. The plane cartwheeled, rolled into a ball, and exploded.

No other incidents stand out in my memories of Williams Field, but, on the whole, it was exciting and challenging.

On November 3, 1943, just seven weeks before my 20th birthday, we graduated from flying school and were rewarded with our silver wings and our commissions as second lieutenants in the U. S. Army Air Force. It was a proud and happy day for me, one that I had never thought that I would see.

After graduation, we were given ten days leave before reporting to our next station. The P38 pilots all went on to operational twin-engine fighter training and then assignment to P38 operational units. Out of the fifty-five of us in Squadron 4, the night fighters, forty-five were sent on to La Junta Army Air Field at La Junta, Colorado, a transition school for B25 pilots, to check out in B25s, prior to night fighter school. The P61, which we were supposed to fly eventually, was actually heavier and had more powerful engines than a B25. Therefore, the rationale was that we should go through B25 transition training to get flying experience in a larger, heavier plane before tackling the P61. Seven of our group were sent to a different B25 school for training as B25 crew members, two returned to Williams Field to instruct in P38s, and one went with those headed for P38 operational units. These last three turned out to be the luckiest ones in our squadron. At least, they were able to continue flying P38s. Had I known what was in store for us, I would have volunteered for P38s myself.

Graduation Day Nov. 3, 1943

I took the train home to Chicago from Phoenix, Arizona. That, in itself, was quite an experience. I had a seat in an old coach that must have been put in mothballs after the Indian wars. Although it was hot on the train, we didn't dare open the windows because of the black, sooty smoke from the engine. (The coaches were obviously built long before air-conditioning was invented!) Many people got on at one station to go to the next (or maybe the second or third one down the line), but they didn't have seats. They had to sit on suitcases in the middle of the aisle. There was no dining car; someone came through with sandwiches and soda pop for sale every once in a while. Sometimes we stopped at a station long enough to hop out and get some fast foods or snacks. After four days of that, I was more than happy to arrive home in Chicago.

Note: between Jan'41 and Aug'45, the total number of aviation cadets accepted for pilot training was **324,647.** Of these, **191,654** were awarded wings (60%). **132,993** (40%) washed out or were killed in training.

5

B25 Transition School

North American B25 Mitchell

La Junta Army Air Field, Colorado

All forty-five of us "intrepid night fighters" returned from leave and checked in at LJAAF ready to learn to fly the B25 before going on to P61 school. We had a few days of orientation, some ground school, and on November 23, 1943, I had my first flight in a B25. I had an hour of dual instruction and rode as a passenger for an hour as the other student had his hour of instruction. This pattern was used extensively in this type of training. For dual instruction (i.e., a flying lesson with an instructor pilot) three persons were in the plane: the instructor pilot and two students. The first student would go through the checklist for starting the plane, taxi out for the first take-off, go through the pre-takeoff procedures, and then begin the flying activities (shooting landings, flying under the hood, etc.). When he had finished his lesson, the two students would exchange places and the second one would take over. This saved time in that they didn't have to taxi in and park the airplane to exchange students. After the second student had finished, he would taxi in, park, and go through the shutdown procedure. (It was up to the instructor to make sure that the next time they flew, it would be turnabout.) The instructor would then pick up two more of his students and go through the whole procedure all over again. I didn't realize it at the time, but this was a pattern that I would go through many times in the future when I became an instructor there myself. "Solo" flights consisted of two students flying the plane, one as pilot, the other as copilot. If they were just practicing take-offs and landings they would land and exchange seats halfway through the period. (One of the fatal accidents we had while I was instructing involved two students who allegedly tried to exchange seats while in flight. One of them apparently stepped on the rudder trim tab control and threw the plane out of control. Neither could get into a seat to recover before the plane crashed.)

I did not fly the next day and for the next six days flew the good old Link trainer. On the last day of the month, I got in another four and a half hours of flying time and qualified for flight pay for the month. At that time, we only needed four hours of pilot time to so qualify. By way of comparison, I was getting the magnificent sum of $150/mo base pay and the flight pay brought it up to $225. That wasn't bad considering that we had received $75/mo as cadets and that GIs were being paid $50/mo.

December started out almost as badly. By the 18th I had five and a half hours of Link trainer time. None of the others in the group were doing much flying either. Then we got the news that changed our world and our hopes for the future. ***The night fighter school was being transferred from Florida to California and they could not take any more pilots for a couple of months. In addition, La Junta was going to be converted from a transition school for B25 pilots to an advanced flying school for aviation cadets!*** The final blow: four out of our class of forty-five were to be put through the B25 transition training in thirty days (it normally took ten weeks) and then be retained as instructors. In addition to myself, my friends Ed Kent, Maurice Fitzgerald, and Joe Foster were the ones picked. We tried to console ourselves with the thought that we were picked because we were the four best pilots in the squadron; actually, we probably did have the best student records in the group, including flying ability and ground school grades. This was very small consolation, however, and that night we drowned our sorrows at the Officers' Club in the biggest drunken party we ever had. Later, when we found out what happened to the others, we realized we were the luckiest in the bunch. The rest of them didn't even get to check out in the B25 and ended up being sent to Troop Carrier Command, where they became copilots in C46s (the huge twin-engine transport known as the Curtis

Commando). After having flown P38s and looking forward to flying P61s, this was getting the shaft in spades.

Don Kelly managed to avoid all of this. He was convinced that it was time to do something else or he would one day find himself on his way into combat. He managed, quite deliberately, to goof up his few flights in the B25 so effectively that he finally was sent to some place in New Mexico or Arizona to fly navigation cadets around for navigation training. That was considered bottom of the barrel to the rest of us but Kelly didn't mind. He didn't plan to do it for very long and I soon had word from him that he was out of the service and collecting a disability pension. I wasn't surprised. He had told me that he was going to do it and offered to help me do the same thing if I went along with him. No way would I even consider such a plan. I loved to fly and was quite happy to fulfill my obligations to the service and to my country in any way that was required as long as I could continue to fly.

A curious incident occurred at home in Chicago about this time. One day the Chicago Tribune reported that 22 Illinois men had been listed as missing in action. Among those listed was a Lt. Robert J. Hornbeck, who lived at 7919 Maryland Avenue in Chicago. My home address was 7610 Maryland Avenue. As an inset to the article, there was a picture box with the pictures of the six missing Chicagoans. One of the pictures was that of me, correctly identified as Lt. R. F. Hornbeck, instead of the other Robert Hornbeck. My mother, knowing I was safely ensconced in La Junta, Colorado, called the newspaper to inform them that they had run the wrong picture. Many of my high school classmates called my mother to find out if I were really missing in action before the error was corrected.

Robert J. Hornbeck was a bombardier on a B17 that was shot down over Germany. He bailed out and was captured by the Germans, but was released at the end of the war. We both returned to college after the war under the G.I. bill and they were forever getting our records mixed up. I talked to him on the phone a couple of times but we never met and eventually both left Chicago.

Getting back to the narrative, on December 19th the four of us selected to become instructors reported to the flight line and flew our tails off for the next thirty-one days. I put in 118 hours of pilot and/or copilot time, eight hours of "passenger" time, and three hours of Link trainer. During this period, there were seven days on which we didn't fly, probably because of bad weather. This comes to an average of over five hours of actual flying time per flying day, all of which was intensive training. We learned to take-off and land the B25 in almost every conceivable configuration, full flaps, partial flaps, no flaps, at night, on instruments, you name it. We had to learn all of the emergency procedures, single-engine operation on instruments, single-engine landings, etc., etc. On January 21st, we reported to the flight line and had four aviation cadets just out of basic flying school assigned to each of us for advanced flying training. It was an awesome responsibility.

The B25 was one of the great planes and probably the best one in which to be an instructor. It had two R-2600-29 Wright Cyclone radial engines that produced 1750 horsepower each on take-off. The propellers were Hamilton Standard Hydromatics, with prop governors and full-feathering capabilities. The planes we flew in training had much of the armor plating removed and no armament, so they were lighter in weight than the operational B25s; officially, they were designated AT24s. It was a very honest airplane, easy to handle, forgiving, and a joy to fly (as medium, twin-engine bombers go). Of course, nothing else I ever flew could top the P38. In my book, that was tops for WWII twin-engine airplanes.

You can imagine the reactions of the students in our first class, that of 44-C. They had less than 150 hours flying time, all in single-engine planes, had flown nothing bigger than a two-seat BT13, with a 450-hp engine, fixed gear, no hydraulic system, and a two-speed prop.

There I stood, not yet a month past my twentieth birthday, with these four trusting students, all older than I was (some by several years). With respect to flying students, **trusting** is the operational word. I always felt that my instructors knew exactly what they were doing and I had complete confidence that, whatever occurred, they could handle it. I suspected that these students felt the same about me, but I didn't at all feel that way about me. So we entered an unspoken (and for them unknown) contract. All five of us would learn together to fly the B25 , except that I would be a few steps ahead of them.

I still remember their names: Phillips, Poe, Pollard, and Pope. Students had been assigned alphabetically, and mine were in the Ps. We had some interesting and exciting times in the next ten weeks, at the end of which they received their silver wings and commissions. I taught several more classes before I left La Junta but remember none of the students in them as well as those in 44-C.

We had transition training, instrument flying, night flying, formation flying, and cross-country flying. One of the night-time cross-country flights stands out in my memory as one of the most memorable flights in my career. It was one night in the middle of February, 1944. I had flown every day for about twelve days in a row and was really tired, but here I was with two students, late at night, on a round-robin flight from La Junta direct to Grand Island, Nebraska, west on the airway to Cheyenne, Wyoming, south on another airway to Pueblo, Colorado, and then east to La Junta. There was some low stratus and ground fog in eastern Colorado, on our way to Grand Island, but it cleared up and the weather was fine at Grand Island. We checked in with the radio range station and gave a position report, then headed west down the airway at 10,000 feet (5,000 ft above the terrain).

In those days, flying an airway on a clear night was like driving down a highway. Every 10-15 miles (depending on the terrain) there were flashing beacons and sometimes you could see three or four beacons down the line. Each beacon had small red lights on the top that could be seen as you flew over it, which flashed six times a minute in Morse code one of ten letters in the alphabet. The pattern would be repeated after every tenth beacon, so it was easy to identify your exact position as you flew over each one. Even to this day, I remember the mnemonic we used to keep track of the order:

When **U**ndertaking **V**ery **H**ard **R**outes **K**eep **D**irections **By** **G**ood **M**ethods

(W,U,V,H,R,K,D,B,G,M)

In addition, you could tune in the beam on the low frequency radio and follow it or tune in the radio range station on the radio compass, which pointed directly at the station. It was virtually impossible to get lost -- or so I thought. When we were settled and on our way to Cheyenne, I put the other student in the right hand seat and told the two of them to follow the airway straight to Cheyenne and to awaken me when we got there. Then I crawled up on the table in the navigator's compartment and went blissfully to sleep.

Some time later, I felt someone shaking my leg and shouting "Sir, wake up, we think we are over Cheyenne." I came to, sat up, and was blinded by a white glare coming through the windshield. We were in clouds, circling at 10,000 feet, with the landing lights on. I quickly climbed into the right-hand seat and turned off the landing lights, so that we could at least see the instrument panel. I asked the student flying the plane why he was flying with the landing lights on and he replied that, since we were in and out of clouds, he turned the lights on to be sure he didn't run into any mountains. I pointed out to him in less than gentle terms that flying in clouds with the landing lights on is one sure way not to see the mountains; all you can see is a white glare. Then I asked him where we were; he pointed down to the spot we were circling, dimly visible just below us, and said that he thought we were over Cheyenne. I looked down and my heart sank. I had flown over Cheyenne at night several times before, and this didn't look anything like it. Moreover, there were no airway beacon lights visible in any direction. I tried tuning in the Cheyenne radio range station and couldn't get anything. In fact, I couldn't get any radio range on the east side of the Rockies. There were thunderstorms in the mountains and the static was severe. I tried Airway Traffic control and got nothing. Slowly, I came to the realization that we were circling at 10,000 feet over some small town west of Cheyenne, but I didn't know where. I did know that there were peaks in the vicinity that went up to 14,000 feet and that we had to be very careful what we did next. I decided to keep circling and climbing to see if we could get on top of the clouds. We got up to 16,000 feet and still hadn't broken through. It was then that I became aware of one of the other insidious effects of hypoxia. Of course, we didn't carry oxygen in these training planes because we were not scheduled for "high-altitude" flights. Actually, I don't think any of our training planes had any oxygen equipment in them. The effect I am referring to is that of loss of night vision. By the time we got up to 16,000 feet, my night vision was so impaired that I could barely make out the instrument panel. This is, one might say, a considerable handicap in flying on instruments at night...

Trying to stay over the lights of the town I could still see dimly through the clouds, we spiraled down to below the cloud deck again, 10,000 feet. I decided on a course of action. I wanted to make my way south and east as much as possible until I could find some way of identifying our position. I didn't dare turn to the east at the start because all was blackness there. In addition, the students didn't know what course we were on when we got to where we were, so it was not a simple matter of just reversing course. I reasoned that if I headed for a light on the ground that there would be no mountain between us and that light. Believe me, there were not many lights on the ground! An occasional farmhouse or a lone automobile or truck traveling late at night was all we had to go by. Nevertheless, we pressed on for some time, working our way from light to light, mostly to the south. Finally I got a fix on the radio range station at Colorado Springs. Although the signal was weak and the static severe, I got a rough bearing of 108 degrees, to the east-southeast. Following lights to the east, we flew 20 minutes to a half hour and, astonishingly, came out over Colorado Springs. To this day, I have not been able to figure out exactly where we were, but we certainly must have been the luckiest air crew in the United States sky, that night. I know that we made our way around some 14,000 foot peaks (including Pike's Peak) and through some mountain passes, but didn't see any of them.

Everything was great when we got to Colorado Springs, the sky was clear, the visibility good, and we headed down the airway to

Pueblo. We got to Pueblo and called in a position report. Pueblo Radio tried to get a message through to me but the static was so bad that I couldn't understand what they were saying, so we headed on course to La Junta. At this point, Pope was flying. A few miles east of Pueblo we hit a solid wall of clouds. The pitot tube iced up immediately and Pope's eyes almost bugged out when he saw the airspeed indicator going rapidly toward zero. I took over the controls, turned on the pitot tube heater, and then turned on the landing lights, which were mounted in the leading edge of the wing, to see if we were picking up ice. At that point I could see a ridge of ice shaped like a two-by-four along the leading edge of the wing. Moreover, our windshield was totally iced over, couldn't see a thing out of it. Immediately, I did a complete 180 and headed back to Pueblo.

By the time we got back to Pueblo, we could see out of the windshield again and I called the tower to cancel my flight plan and asked for landing instructions. It was now about 0200 in the morning and there wasn't much traffic about, so they cleared me for a straight-in approach. As I prepared for the landing and reduced my speed for the final approach glide of 120 mph, the plane started dropping like a rock. I had to bring it in at about 140 mph indicated airspeed all the way to the ground. The Pueblo field was at about 5000 feet of altitude, so the plane was actually doing about 160 mph when I set her down. I made sure we landed close to the end of the runway so that we would have plenty of room in which to stop. On top of everything else, the tower had mentioned that there were icy spots on the runway. We got stopped O.K. and taxied in. We parked the plane and they put the three of us up in the BOQ. The message Pueblo Radio had tried to get through to us was that La Junta was socked in and that we would have to land at Pueblo. We found it out the hard way.

That night I had the worst nightmare I have ever had. I was in a B25 with two students and we were lost in the mountains at night. No matter what we did, we couldn't get out of the mountains and there was no place to land. I woke up in a cold sweat, relieved to discover that we were on the ground. It was curious that I had not felt any fear when we were actually lost in the mountains, only a concern and a determination to see it through. But the fear did come out in the dream.

The next morning, after breakfast, the weather had cleared and we prepared to fly the 60 miles to La Junta. Checking the plane, we saw that the two-by-four of ice was present on all of the leading edges of the wings and tail surfaces. I forgot to mention that not only did our training planes have no oxygen equipment, we didn't have any deicers, either. That was why I made such a quick and frantic turn when we started picking up ice. So, the three of us were out there chopping ice off the plane. I was glad we had done that when we took off for La Junta. We got into the air O.K., but a B26 taking off right after us, which apparently had not had the ice chopped off, crashed and burned on the take-off, killing all on board.

After we got back to La Junta, I visited the weather station to see if I could figure out what had happened the night before. It turned out that a "closed low" had developed at 10,000 feet over the Great Plains and that we actually had a modest tail wind on our flight west, instead of the slight head wind we had been told to expect. (A closed low means that the wind pattern had developed a completely counter-clockwise movement, resulting in easterly flow of air over Colorado.) Because of this, our ground speed was higher than anticipated and we reached Cheyenne much sooner than we had thought. The students were flying by the clock instead of their heads and didn't identify Cheyenne when we passed over it, but kept on going. That was how we ended up so far west of it but I still don't know where we were for certain. We all learned something from that experience. As for myself, never again did I crawl into the navigator's compartment and go to sleep on the table while the students did the flying.

My experiences with hypoxia were not yet at an end. (I guess I was just a slow learner, or maybe obstinate. My wife would go for obstinate.) One day after shooting landings until we were tired of it, I decided to see how high we could go in the B25. One time in basic I had a BT13 up to 18,000 feet, but it didn't have any superchargers and was just clawing the sky to stay in the air at that altitude. We had two-speed superchargers on the B25, low-blower for low altitude flight and high-blower for high-altitude flight. It took 225 hp on each engine to run the blowers in high, so it wasn't something you used until you really needed the increased manifold pressure. Anyway, we managed to get up to 26,000 feet, which I thought was great. Then I had another great idea (but this one was induced by hypoxia). I decided it would be really fun to try a slow roll in a B25, and my students enthusiastically agreed (they weren't on oxygen either...). Over we went but when I got it upside-down I couldn't continue the roll. Moreover, everything loose fell to the ceiling; no one had ever inverted that plane before. I had sense enough at that point to chop the throttles, pull back on the stick, and split-S out of it. We pulled out at about 10,000 feet with the airspeed indicator banging on the red line (425 mph indicated). The two students with me that day decided that the B25 wasn't really an acrobatic plane and I had to agree with them.

On another occasion I flew to Amarillo, Texas to bring back two of my students who had landed there while on a cross-country flight because of a problem with their plane. The weather was not great, much cloudiness and some storms in the area. I had to file an instrument flight plan for the return trip and flew TOVC. (That means that you are cleared to fly 500' on top of the overcast, but cannot penetrate the clouds without additional clearance to let down through them.) When we were in the vicinity of La Junta, at about 12,000 feet, I could see that a line of thunderstorms was lying right down the beam, through which I would have to let down. I called traffic control and the La Junta control tower and found there was no one else in the air in the vicinity of La Junta -- it really was a bad day for flying. I told the tower that I was going to let down for landing but that I couldn't do a routine descent because of the thunderstorms, which they happily acknowledged. Spotting a hole in the cloud deck below us, I spiraled down through it and found myself between layers. I did this several times and soon found that I could see the ground and was about 500 feet above our auxiliary field at Rocky Ford. Knowing exactly the course and distance to the main field, I called the tower, gave them my location, and received clearance for a straight-in approach. We were in and out of low fragmented clouds (called "scud") and it was raining heavily. During the letdown and the approach to the field, frequent flashes of lightning occurred; each time there was a flash of lightning, I would get a shock through the control column. This was the only time I ever experienced anything like that, and it was rather distracting under the circumstances. Finally, I looked down through the rain and the scud and saw that we were passing directly over the main field. I informed the tower, dropped the gear and flaps, cut back the throttles, and spiraled down for a landing. I was glad to be on the ground; there was no way I could have made a normal instrument descent through all of the thunderstorm activity; the way I chose was more fun, anyway. There are times when the optimism of youth is a positive asset.

Well, Phillips, Poe, Pollard, and Pope survived my instruction and learned to fly the B25 well enough to graduate in the class of 44-C. I had five students in the next class, 44-E, four of whose names began with N but I don't remember them. The fifth student was an older fellow whose name was Nate Owens; he was a gem, the best student I ever had. Unfortunately, he was shot down in a B29 raid over Tokyo on his third mission. He left a wife and two small children.

My last class at La Junta was 44-I. By this time, they must have been scraping the bottom of the barrel. These students had flown Cessna AT17s in basic training, also known as the "Bamboo Bomber." It was not much of a plane; it had twin 225-hp engines with carved wooden propellers. It was possible to slow-fly the plane at about 30 mph, turn off one engine, and have the propeller come to a complete stop. It is the only twin-engine plane I've ever seen in which you could get a fixed-pitch propeller to stop completely in mid-air by shutting down one engine. I had to take a refresher instrument training course at La Junta in the middle of the summertime in the AT17. In rough air, the plane bobbed around like a cork in rough water. It was the most difficult under-the-hood flying I ever did. The instruments would swing widely and wildly from one reading to another and you just tried to get the average to come out to what you wanted.

The students I had in the class of 44-I didn't seem to know what a needle and ball were for, or what coordination was. They had been able to slop through flying in the AT17 to the point that I practically had to teach them the basics of flying all over again. It was tough going but by this time I had enough experience instructing that I got them through it O.K., but not without one incident that was as close as I ever want to be to boring a deep hole in the ground.

It was decided by higher authority, and probably by someone who had never instructed in B25s, that we should instill confidence in our students in the stability of the B25 in single-engine flight by demonstrating a single-engine stall. A plane "stalls" when the speed is low enough and the angle at which the wing meets the air is steep enough that the airflow over the wing is no longer smooth, but turbulent. At this point, the wing loses lift, the ailerons become ineffective, and the plane starts to drop. In order to overcome this, it is necessary to lower the nose of the airplane and give the engines more power to increase the speed. You can do this maneuver with the power off (a power-off stall) or with some power on (a power-on stall) and we always had students practice these maneuvers to become familiar with the stall characteristics of the airplane. A stall while close to the ground or turning on the final approach in making a landing can result in a fatal crash, and has killed many students and fledgling pilots.

A single-engine stall is something else again. In this maneuver, one engine is shut down or simulated dead, while power still remains on the good engine. If the plane is stalled in these circumstances, the wing with the dead engine will stall out before the other wing and the plane will fall off on the wing with the dead engine. If you attempt to bring the wing up using aileron control, it exacerbates the condition, making the stall worse on the low wing and reducing it on the high. Consequently, the bank steepens and the plane can go into a tailspin. It is absolutely necessary to try to lessen the angle of bank by using the rudder controls, which can be done, and to overcome the natural tendency of a pilot to crank in aileron.

Knowing all of this, I took my two students out to demonstrate the maneuver and give them confidence in the single-engine flying ability of the B25. We climbed up to 11,000 feet (6,000 feet above the ground), went through the maneuver, and the wing dropped off dramatically. I dropped the nose, used rudder to pick up the wing, and we were flying again. The student in the left seat was so impressed that he asked if he could try it, so I said he could, cautioning him against using aileron in the recovery. Up came the nose, the plane shuddered, started falling off on the side of the dead engine, and the next thing I knew we were in the flattest and fastest tailspin I have ever seen. He had cranked in full aileron. I hollered "I've got it," took over the controls, and tried conventional spin recovery. Airflow over the twin rudders was so strong that I couldn't budge the rudder with all my pressure on the pedal, even with the student helping out. I dumped the control column forward and was able to steepen up the spin, and finally got the rudders to respond. I broke the spin and started pulling back on the control column to recover from the dive we were in. As I attempted to pull out, we hit a high-speed stall, and went into a secondary spin. At this point I discovered that the student had cranked in full rudder trim tab to help hold the plane straight while approaching the stall -- something else he wasn't supposed to do. I remember looking over at the airspeed indicator and the altimeter. We were doing 180 mph and the altimeter was unwinding like I couldn't believe. Knowing how I had broken out of the spin before, I used the same technique, stopped the spin, cranked off the rudder trim tab so I wouldn't have to hold opposite rudder, and eased out of the dive. We pulled out about 600 feet above the ground doing about 450 mph indicated airspeed. At the rate we had been losing altitude, that 600 feet was about two seconds worth of additional tailspin. They say that your life flashes before your eyes before you crash. Don't you believe it! I was so busy trying to recover from that spin that we could have gone straight into the ground before I had time to reflect on anything.

Having exceeded the allowed limits on the airplane and having scared the wits out of ourselves in addition, I judiciously headed straight back to the field and called in for an emergency landing, not being sure a wing or one of the tail surfaces wouldn't fall off at any moment. We got on the ground O.K., taxied in, parked, shut down the engines, and got out of the plane. I started to walk away and that's when it hit me. My legs just seemed to turn to rubber and I almost fell down. I managed to make it into the ready room, but was a mite shaky. I reported to our squadron C.O. what had happened and learned that one of the other instructors had a similar experience. The next day the order requiring simulated single-engine stalls was rescinded, and we all breathed easier. I felt fortunate to be able to breathe at all.

One additional incident involving the class of 44-I illustrates my frustration and the fact that I was ready to move on to something else. I had two of the students up for single-engine landings. To simulate an engine failure, you pull the throttle back on one engine while the student is engaged in something else. It is up to him to take whatever corrective action is necessary to continue his flight. In an actual engine failure he would feather the prop, cut off the switch and fuel to the dead engine, and trim the plane for single-engine flight. Instead of feathering the prop in a training exercise, we simply adjusted the throttle on the "dead" engine to 15 inches of mercury manifold pressure and kept it running. At that power setting, the propeller would "stream-line" so that it would not produce any thrust or any drag, but the engine would not get cold. One of the things I tried to drill into the students was that the B25 could not sustain its altitude in flight on one engine if the landing gear was down. In a single-engine landing, you did not extend the landing gear until you were committed to the runway and certain that you were going to make it.

With one of the students in the left seat, we entered the traffic pattern at an auxiliary field to shoot a landing. The usual procedure was to enter the pattern 1500' above the ground on an overhead approach in line with the runway, slow the plane, drop the landing gear, and go through the pre-landing check list. You then made a 180 degree turn to the left, dropping 500 feet so that you were at 1000 feet on the downwind leg. A little past the landing end of the runway, you turned on the base leg, dropping another 500 feet so that you were at 500 feet turning on the final approach. We were turning onto the downwind leg and I cut an engine off (engine failure does not necessarily occur at a convenient time). The student did all of the right things but forgot to raise the landing gear. Our speed kept dropping until it got as low as he dared, then our altitude started dropping. When we reached the point to turn onto the base leg, we were only 300 feet above the ground, our airspeed was at a minimum, and he started the turn. In an actual situation, we never would have completed that turn but would have dug a big hole in the ground. In disgust, I shouted "I've got it," took over the controls, raised the landing gear, and got us out of there. What got to me was not the fact that he forgot to raise the landing gear, but that he didn't even try to figure out why he couldn't keep up his speed and altitude, but blithely continued on in an increasingly dangerous situation. There are no old, bold pilots, but neither are there any old, stupid pilots.

One of the duties we had occasionally was to serve as tower officer during night flying. Instructor pilots would be assigned to this duty, like drawing K.P. The tower officer would be in the control tower with the tower operators and was responsible for whatever was going on. It was also his responsibility to call off local flying if conditions warranted it.

One night while I was tower officer, we had about 50 B25s out for local night flying. It was a clear, cold night -- perfect conditions for the formation of ground fog. About 0400 a plane on the final approach called to say that ground fog was forming near the end of the runway. I immediately called off flying and all planes were notified to return to base, and boy, did they return! There were B25s all over the sky. At one time I counted 14 planes lined up on the final approach to the runway. The third from last plane in the air called on the final approach to say that the runway was obscured by fog, so he and the other two had to go to Pueblo. That was one night I was happy to be on the ground and not up in the air.

Paul (Ed) Kent, Fitzgerald (whom we called Fitzgeezel), Joe Foster, and I became very good friends and had a lot of fun flying together. Once in a while we would get a couple of BT13s or AT6s and fly up to Denver for a weekend. Sometimes we would meet in our B25s to demonstrate the plane's capabilities to our students by doing a little mock "dog fighting" or just fly on top of cloud decks, skimming the surface of the clouds and following their up and down contours, sometimes down the canyons formed by towering cumulus clouds. (Highly illegal activities but great fun.)

Alan Bufkin (Buff) joined our squadron as an instructor and also became a good friend. We were assigned two to a room in the BOQ and Ed and I shared a room throughout our stay. (Room it was only in a broad sense; it didn't even have a door on it. The latrine was in a separate building, which didn't encourage getting up and going to the bathroom on a cold winter night.) Ed and I had been together since primary school at Oxnard and were almost the same age. I think I was just a month older than he was. Buff was a great guy, a few years older than we were, and lived off the base with his wife, Betty. She became a good friend to us, also.

Joe Foster actually came from a little town close to La Junta called Las Animas, where we had one of our auxiliary fields. An auxiliary field consisted of three intersecting runways out in the middle of nowhere with a control tower and not much else. It was used just for practicing take-offs and landings. We had two of them, one at Las Animas and one at Rocky Ford, the place where the great cantaloupes come from. Anyway, Joe had Ed, Fitzgeezel, and me over to his folks' ranch one weekend and we did some rabbit hunting. Another time we were driving in to town in Joe's 1935 Ford, with a cloth top (but it was not a convertible), when we got caught in a violent hailstorm. Joe pulled off the road and stopped as we huddled on the floor of the car with hailstones coming right through the cloth top and the cloth interior to fall somewhat harmlessly on top of us. In a few minutes hail was about three inches deep on the road. Then, almost as abruptly, it stopped and cleared up.

When we got back to the base we saw an AT11 that had been caught in the same hailstorm and made an emergency landing. The windshield was totally smashed in and the leading edges of the wings and tail surfaces were bashed inward as though they had battered by a thousand ball-peen hammers. Those were two lucky guys who managed to get that plane on the ground and survive.

We didn't go into town much. It was a small town, population about 5,000, with one movie theater that showed films in Spanish, half a dozen or so western-type bars, and a few uninspiring restaurants. Consequently, most of the places in town were off limits to officers so that the enlisted personnel would have at least a few places to go. Our social lives revolved around the Officers' Club on the base, but that wasn't much to be proud of either. At least it gave us a place to sit around and have a few drinks, and on Saturday nights they usually had a small band and some of the guys would have their wives there for dancing.

Every opportunity that we had, the five of us (and many of the others) would volunteer for combat duty. We had about 150 B25s at La Junta, about 75 of which were available for flying on any given day. During the period I was there, we lost an average of two planes a month in fatal crashes, usually one "solo" plane (with two students only), and one "dual" (an instructor and two students). Causes of the crashes varied a great deal, but the statistics relentlessly continued on. Many of us felt that we would like to have at least one crack at the enemy before we "bought the farm" and so we volunteered.

One of the accidents hit me hard, personally. I had developed a friendship with a fellow instructor by the name of Tommy LeClair. One afternoon a group of us were in the base theater for some kind of a lecture when were heard the loud noise of a prop running away, followed by the sound of a crash, and the lights going off in the theater. We all hurried out and rushed toward the flight line, just a few hundred yards away. A B25 had a runaway prop on takeoff, turned 180 degrees in a very sharp turn, and crashed in between some buildings on the edge of the runway. When a propeller governor fails and the prop "runs away," it goes to flat pitch and becomes a total drag on the plane. It is impossible to continue flying in that condition and it is imperative to cut the power immediately and belly in straight ahead. The instructor had allowed the students to fly as pilot and copilot, while he stood behind and between the seats to observe them. When the prop ran away, there was nothing he could do to control the plane, and when it hit the ground he was thrown right through the canopy onto the road. It must have broken every major bone in his body. When they picked his body up it was as limp as a rag doll. It was my friend, Tommy.

One day my students and I were approaching the auxiliary field at Rocky Ford to shoot some landings. As we were about to enter the traffic pattern, there was the flash of the underside of a fuselage caught in the sunlight, as a B25 headed down in a precipitous angle. We held our breath, but there was no pullout and it went straight into the ground. It also was a dual flight and no one ever figured out what had happened. I had some anxious moments wondering which of the guys in our squadron it was, but it turned out to be one of the fellows I hadn't known very well and was less of a personal loss (to me, that is). But a very personal loss to those who loved him.

There was a B24 training base at Pueblo and we would frequently see the four-engine guys lumbering around the area. One day my students and I were near the western edge of our local flying area and again caught the flash of sunlight as a plane headed earthward. It was a B24 from Pueblo. There was quite a fireball when it hit; makes one think serious thoughts about how transient life is, even at the tender age of twenty.

One happy day near the end of August 1944, a bunch of us received orders to report to the pilot replacement pool in Columbia, South Carolina, for assignment to B25J combat crews. We were ready to go and none of us had the slightest misgiving about leaving La Junta. However, I have always felt that was where I really learned to fly. On or about September 6th we were on our way to Columbia.

A few days after we checked in at the pilot pool in Columbia, several of us were at the flight line looking at the transient planes parked there and we saw these great looking twin-engine attack planes called A20 Havocs. They were built by Douglas and had been exported to England and France (before we got in the war) as DB7s, or Bostons, as they were designated for the British and the

French. (There was also a night fighter version called the P70, but it was being replaced by the P61 "Black Widow," the plane that I was destined never to fly.) We got excited talking about the A20s and about how neat it would be to get into them instead of B25Js. One of the fellows in our group said "Well, why not?" and we looked at him somewhat bemused. It so happened that he had a friend who was a top sergeant in the Headquarters Office where orders were cut assigning pilots in the pool. He took a quart of whiskey over to him and explained our situation. We were amazed and delighted a week or two later when we received orders sending us to Morris Field, Charlotte, North Carolina for A20 transition training. It has forever boggled my mind that the gift of one quart of whiskey could have had such a profound effect on the rest of my life and the thirteen others with me.

We parted company with Fitzgerald and Foster at that point. They had elected to stay in B25s and go on as our original orders had specified. I learned later that Fitzgerald was killed when his plane was shot down in Italy. It is my understanding that the B25s had to attack the Germans by flying single file through a mountain pass and they nailed the planes as they came through one at a time. I don't know what happened to Joe Foster; never heard any more from or about him.

6

A20 Transition School

Douglas A20H Havoc

Morris Field, Charlotte, N.C.

As an introduction to my experiences at Morris Field, I would like to quote from a letter I wrote home to my mother and father on October 23, 1944, shortly after I got there.

"This is really a fine spot here. I'm going to enjoy these next three months quite a bit. The base is swell, small, well-kept, everybody friendly, etc., all the little things that go to make up a good post. The BOQs are wonderful --- Ed and I are sharing a room -- they are of permanent construction, with inside latrines (quite an important factor in the winter time, and believe me it has been cold lately), a central heating system, wooden floors and real walls and doors (we had cement floors and plasterboard walls at La Junta). To top it off, the Officers' Club is the most beautiful I've seen on any post, the food is swell and very reasonable (65 to 70 cents for an average meal). All in all, this post has my vote for the 'one I'd least hate to be an instructor at.'

The town is pretty nice, too. About as big or bigger than Columbia but hardly any soldiers, only fellows from the air base. Ed and I went to church last night at the biggest and most beautiful Methodist church I've ever seen. The Methodists are doing all right down here.

We got here late Friday afternoon, were assigned to quarters, etc., processed all day Saturday, went into town Saturday night (got there quite late, barely had time to eat supper and make the late show). After the show we just stood around knocking ourselves out at all the civilians (mostly girls) on the street. We slept rather late Sunday (until about two), missed dinner, missed the football game, to sum it up, we just missed the boat. Interesting fact -- all of the movie houses in town close from six until nine on Sunday evening -- so that people will go to church.

This morning we had ground school from 8 until noon, had lunch, and went down to the flight line at one. To our surprise, we had to fly. There is a minimum of so many hours that we must acquire in the right seat of a B25 before checking out in an A20. (Note: this was no sweat for us B25 instructors. Most of us had forgotten how to fly a B25 from the left seat!) Also we must have certain subjects in ground school on the fuel, hydraulic, electrical, and emergency systems before flying it. Anyhow, I went up with an instructor, looked over the local area, shot a couple of landings, and that's all there was to it. Should start flying A20s about Thursday or Friday.

By the way, I already have a crew picked out. They got in Friday night, too, and Saturday we looked over their records for fellows from home. I got two gunners, one a flight engineer, the other an armorer. The first is a young fellow about 22 from Bloomington, Ind., a quiet, soft-spoken, redheaded kid by the name of James Lawrence. The second is a kid about 20, and he's from 87th and Halsted, went to Calumet. (Note: this was about three miles from where I grew up in Chicago. Calumet was a rival high school and was the place I actually had my high school graduation ceremony because the auditorium at Hirsch (the school I went to) was being worked on at the time). His name is Leroy Harris. They're both corporals. They were glad to hear I had so much (pilot) time and experience; after all, they take a pretty big chance sitting there in the back with their lives entrusted entirely to the hands of the pilot, helpless to do anything if he makes a wrong move. (Note: unlike other twin-engine bombers, the A20 had a narrow fuselage and carried only one pilot, no copilot. Also, the gunners in the rear of the fuselage were totally cut off from the pilot's cockpit; the only communication was through the intercom). We start flying together when I finish the first phase, about four weeks. We have an awfully small class, only eighteen crews. Usually there are forty or fifty. They say some of the instructors here will be shipping out with us when we go to combat. Could be."

The contrast with La Junta in living conditions certainly impressed me, as well as the comparatively pleasant conditions in town. All of that was secondary to the reason we were at Morris Field: to learn to fly the A20. It soon took its place in my heart as second only to the P38. It was a great little plane and was finally supplanted by its "big brother" the Douglas A26 late in the war, although we were flying combat missions in the A20s right up to the very end of the war.

The A20G (with the solid nose and no bombardier) and the A20J (with the bombardier's compartment in the nose) had Wright Cyclone R-2600-23 engines with a take-off rating of 1600 hp. The later models, the H and K respectively, had the same engines as the B25s we had flown, the R-2600-29, rated at 1750 hp. Gross weight of the A20 in combat configuration was about 24,000 lb, whereas the B25 was 35,000 to 40,000 lb, so it is easy to see why the A20 was a hotter and faster plane.

Flying the A20 was more like flying a fighter again. There was no copilot and so you had only yourself to rely on. As with the P38, it was possible to squeeze someone behind the pilot for a piggy-back ride. In the A20 there was a long, shallow place behind the pilot that was the top of the bomb bay, where the life raft was usually stowed. By removing the life raft, it was possible for someone to lie flat on his belly with his head over the pilot's shoulder to observe flying procedures. This was done before you were turned loose to fly the plane solo and at least gave you an inkling of how the plane behaved in various flight attitudes.

My first solo flight in the A20 was not as spectacular as it was in the P38, but I fell in love with it immediately. It was truly a pilot's airplane, responsive, maneuverable, easy on the controls, and full of zip. It was especially a delight to fly at low altitude, for which it was specifically designed. The high power to weight ratio, short fuselage, and unique wing design made it the fastest and most maneuverable plane at sea level through much of World War II. (For those who are interested, the outer portions of the wing had a shallower angle of incidence than the inner wing. At high speed, most of the lift would come from the inner wing, while the outer wing was "stream-lined" and produced little lift but also very little drag. At low speed, the inner wing -- being at a higher angle of attack -- would stall out before the outer, which gave you more lift and better aileron control at lower speeds than if the entire wing stalled at the same time.) The short fuselage and low wing loading gave it an extraordinary ability to "hedge-hop," which was extremely useful in low-level skip bombing and strafing. It could hop up and down over ground obstacles at speeds that would have had a B25 hitting high-speed stalls or mushing into the trees.

Our course of instruction involved all of the usual things, transition training, formation flying, instrument and night flying, etc. However, we did have greater emphasis on low-level flying and low-level navigation. We had a minimum altitude of 200 feet that we were supposed to observe, a rule that was observed more in the breach than in the compliance. We also did a lot of low-level formation flying, which reminds me of one of the wildest flights I was ever on.

It was New Year's Day, 1945. We had brought the New Year in with a truly memorable party, except that none of us could remember it. I got back to the dormitory about six in the morning, flopped on the bed, and fell asleep instantly. At 0700, we were awakened and told to report to the flight line at 0800. After an unenthusiastic breakfast, we made it to the flight line on time and were given the schedule for the day. When the operations officer looked at the raggle-taggle, hung-over pilots standing in front of him, he released all gunners for the day with some comment about it being inhuman to be required to face the hazards of flight with pilots in such a state. However, since the war must go on and the airplanes must be flown, no pilots were excused.

When I saw the schedule, I was devastated. I was scheduled for low-level formation flying. It was a crisp, clear winter morning with a strong wind blowing. Hedge-hopping over the rolling hills of North Carolina is always a challenge, but to do it in formation, in this kind of wind, and in the condition I was in -- my mind just boggled at the thought. There was no sympathy, no respite, no alternative. Off we went, the other student and I, flying on the instructor's wing in the loosest formation I have ever seen. The turbulence was awe-inspiring; at least, it inspired awe in me. It was an hour and a half of fighting the controls constantly while turning and twisting our way over the hills. Finally, we headed back to the field and peeled off, entering the traffic pattern to land. The instructor peeled off first, then each of us in turn. As I came around in the pattern, I suddenly thought: *the instructor's in worse shape than I am!* Here we were, preparing to land on the very short runway, about half the length of the other two, one that we never used. I called in on the final approach and checked with the tower that I was coming in on the correct runway. (Remember the crazy sonofabitch with the red flag in primary?) Well, I was coming in on the correct runway, and I landed in the strongest head wind I'd ever experienced in a landing. The wind was fierce and blowing straight down the runway; it would have been madness to have tried landing on either of the other runways because of the intense cross wind. We all survived the morning's escapades, but I don't think any of us who were in the air that morning forgot the experience.

The A20G and H had a twin-gun Martin turret and we had to go to Myrtle Beach with our gunners to give them practice in firing the twin .50-cal machine guns. They were used mostly for defensive firepower in the event of attack by enemy planes. Under some circumstances, the gunners could use the guns for strafing in a low-level attack, so they had training in both modes. It was fun for the pilots because all we had to do was follow the prescribed maneuvers and give the gunners a chance to do their thing. I'm sure the gunners enjoyed the experience, too; I would have.

Myrtle Beach was a fascinating airfield. The runways and taxiways were hacked out of a forest, with trees everywhere. It was possible to be taxiing out to the active runway and not be able to see anything but trees on either side of the plane. In some situations, you could be sitting near the end of the runway, ready to pull out onto the runway for take-off, and not be able to see the control tower. It gave one a queasy feeling; if you couldn't see them, they couldn't see you. It required a great deal of faith in the clarity and accuracy of radio communications under those circumstances.

The story was told at the base of the A20 that landed, started taxiing in, and then disappeared among the trees. The pilot got all mixed up on the taxi strip and finally called in to the tower for instructions on how to get to the parking area. The tower operator asked him where he was and he replied that he was in front of the base theater! Seems he had turned off the taxi strip onto a road and that's where he ended up. There must not have been much vehicular traffic on the road that day...Back at Morris Field, we had an exciting incident when a B17 came in for an emergency landing in bad weather. He overshot the runway and landed way long, couldn't stop the plane, went past the end, sheared off his landing gear, and came to rest right on top of a railroad track. An express passenger train was due at any moment and a railroad employee grabbed a broom, doused it with gasoline, lit it, and went running down the railroad track frantically waving the flaming broom. The engineer saw it through the fog and brought the train to a stop not too far from the plane. It was almost like an episode from a Saturday afternoon kids' serial at the movies. It would have been a total disaster if the train had hit the B17. They had to cut the plane in half to get it off the track so the train could continue.

Strange things happen in training. We had an A20 come in from a local flight in bad weather one time; one of the guys in our class was flying it but I can't remember his name. It was raining, the runway was slick, and he ran off the runway into the soft dirt. The nose wheel collapsed and the plane flipped over on its back. There was no fire and someone got over to the plane, stooped down, and asked the pilot if he was O.K. He replied that he was and was told not to release his seat belt and shoulder straps until the emergency guys could get there to help him, so he wouldn't fall on his head. Again, he acknowledged the message. When the emergency team arrived, he appeared to be unconscious. When they cut through to him and got him out of the plane, he was dead. There were no physical injuries and the eventual medical diagnosis was that his heart had failed. It was strange. Perhaps he went into shock and his heart couldn't take the strain in that position.

I mentioned the gunnery training for the aircrew, but the most fun was the gunnery and skip-bombing for the pilots. The A20 had six .50-cal guns in the nose and bomb racks in the bomb bay and under the wings. Fortunately the guns were charged hydraulically, so there was no repeat of my near-disaster in the AT6 gunnery incident. We fired live ammunition in all six guns for strafing practice and dropped 100-lb bombs containing 5-lb spotting charges for bombing practice. We soon were able to drop bombs on low-level runs within 25-50 feet of the target. We also had a couple of missions using chemical tanks mounted on the wing racks to simulate laying a smoke screen or dispersing chemicals. For these missions, collection papers were laid out in the target area and we flew over at low level with a colored, sticky liquid in the tanks. The fraction of papers covered with the dispersant was a measure of the accuracy of delivery.

We also did some low-level cross-country flying to develop our skills in pilotage, navigating with a map in our laps and looking for roads, railroad tracks, bridges, etc. to keep on course. This led to an amusing incident somewhat reminiscent of the time the instructor bailed out of the BT13 in primary. We were headed toward the flight line and someone said, "Look, there's a parachute coming down." It was a gunner who had been riding in the back while his pilot was on a low-level cross country. The pilot was returning to the base at 200 feet and suddenly saw the field directly in front of him. He pulled back hard on the control column and climbed quickly to 1000 feet so he would be in the traffic pattern. The gunner, not being able to see what the pilot was up to, feared the plane was out of control and bailed out! I would say that he had rather less than complete confidence in his pilot's ability. I'm not sure whether that crew stayed together or not. I suspect not.

Occasionally while out on local flying, Ed and I would meet and have a mock dogfight in our A20s; it was much more fun than it was in B25s, almost like flying in fighters. One day we were both scheduled for cross country navigation flights. I took off before Ed and waited for him. As he came up, flying on course, I did a wingover and made a pass at him, but he didn't respond. I did another wingover and tried it a second time, but again no response. I couldn't understand why he was ignoring me, but I went on my way. When I got back to the ready room, there was the inevitable message for me, "Report to the C.O.'s office immediately!" I knocked, entered, saluted, and once more was accosted by an instructor and the Squadron C.O. I was accused of buzzing another aircraft and of exceeding the allowed angle of bank in a plane that had a Martin turret (some of the older models didn't have the turret). I was told that you were not to exceed 75 degrees of bank in a plane with a turret and that I had been observed flying at an angle of about 105 degrees. I guess they were pretty steep wingovers. Pleading guilty to all of the above but claiming that I hadn't known about the restriction on banking, I was given another chewing out and dismissed. When I talked to Ed about the incident, he said that he had seen the instructor taking off right after him and thought that he might be watching, so he decided to lie low. It was just as well; if he hadn't, we might have gotten into even worse trouble.

We finished our training and about the middle of January 1945 were transferred with our crews to Hunter Field, Georgia for outfitting and preparation for overseas assignment. Most of us were assigned to the Pacific theatre and were sent by train to Camp Stoneman, outside of Pittsburg, California for shipment to the Southwest Pacific Area (SWPA). The A20s didn't have sufficient range to fly across, so the planes and crews were sent by ship.

Kent, Bufkin, and I were still together, along with Rifkin, Blue, Woodleton, and several others whose names I don't remember. We ended up on this great U.S. Army Transport ship, the General H. W. Butner. Since it belonged to the army, it was manned by Coast Guard personnel. It carried 6,500 troops and we left San Francisco on February 17th, bound for Finschhafen, New Guinea.

It was a fast ship and traveled alone, maintaining about 23 knots cruising speed and zig-zagging its way across the Pacific. We did not have plush accommodations; we had twelve officers in a small cabin just big enough for twelve bunks stacked three high with six on each side of the cabin.. The enlisted men were packed in with bunks 5 high; they barely had enough room between bunks to turn over. The officers were given three meals a day in the wardroom, but the GIs only had two meals a day and spent most of their time standing in line for them.

Every morning we were awakened by a bugle blast on the loudspeaker. Shortly after that would come the announcement "Sweepers, man your brooms! Sweep down fore and aft." (I don't know if they did that routinely on Naval vessels or if this was something the Coast Guard cooked up to needle the Army.) A little later, it would be "Testing, whistle and siren. Testing, whistle and siren." Then would come several loud blasts of the whistle that probably could be heard by Japanese submarines in Tokyo Bay, followed by a whoop, whoop, whooping of the siren that was not a whit lower in volume. After all of this, it was about time for target practice, and the 3-inch anti-aircraft guns and 40-mm pompoms would let loose with a racket that could almost have raised the dead from Davy Jones' locker, a mile or two below us. Every night, one half hour before sunset, all troops were sent below and the hatches closed. They remained closed until half an hour after sunrise. There was no lying about on deck watching the stars at night. This was not what you would call an idyllic ocean cruise.

On February 25th we crossed the equator at 1345. I was engaged in our usual activity at the time, playing pinochle. We didn't gamble or play poker but we did enjoy pinochle. The next day we crossed the dateline, which confused us no end for several days.

We passed through the Solomon Islands and saw Guadalcanal; it was the first land we had seen since leaving San Francisco. We arrived at Finschhafen on March 4th. For some strange reason, the aircrews, who were headed for Nadzab just a few miles up the valley from Lae, about 70 miles east of Finschhafen, did not disembark. Instead, they kept us on the ship and proceeded on up the coast to Hollandia. Between Finschhafen and Hollandia there were some 30,000 Japanese troops cut off in the area around Wewak. During the night, as we passed Wewak, a Japanese submarine lying offshore spotted the ship in the moonlight and fired two torpedoes at it. The Butner had a very shallow draft for the size of the ship and the torpedoes were set too deep. They passed directly below the ship and didn't detonate. With over 6,000 men below decks and the hatches closed, we wouldn't have stood a chance if the ship had been sunk. Even if we had made it to shore, the Japanese troops were there to welcome us with their bayonets.

The next day we arrived at Hollandia and disembarked. It was wild to see these pilots and crews all decked out in helmets, packs, shoulder holsters, and leggings, climbing down the nets on the side of the ship into landing craft that were pitching and tossing in the water below. I remarked at the time that we looked like a bunch of paddlefeet (a somewhat less than endearing term for ground officers).

7

Combat in the Southwest Pacific Area (SWPA)

Nadzab CRTC

We were assigned to the Far Eastern Air Force (FEAF) Combat Replacement Training Center (CRTC), which had its own A20s and instructor pilots for training crews in combat roles. A20 crews from the States were given four combat missions with combat-experienced crews leading, and then were assigned to one of the three operational A20 groups in the FEAF: the 312th Bomb Group on Luzon, the 417th Bomb Group on Mindoro, and the 3rd Bomb Group, also on Mindoro.

The north coast of New Guinea (Hollandia) was no tropical paradise. The weather was hot and muggy; the air was so humid that you had to build a fire to dry out your socks after they were washed. One day we went off on a hike and found a beautiful stream in the nearby hills that spilled down over some rocks and made little bathing pools in the rocks at the base. We had great fun playing in the water; it was really warm.

There were many destroyed Japanese planes on the ground at Hollandia, remnants of the big air strike conducted by the Fifth Air Force against the Japanese base there just a year before. By actual count, the Japanese lost 240 planes on the ground. B24s of the 22nd and 90th Bomb groups struck for several days in a row, and the coup de grace was administered by 96 A20s of the 3rd and 312th Groups, followed by 76 B25s from the 38th and 345th Groups. Escort and fighter cover was provided by 36 P38s from the 431st and 433rd Squadrons. During this action Major Richard Bong shot down his 27th and 28th planes, beating Eddie Rickenbacker's record from World War I.

On March 13th we were packed aboard C47s and flown back

to Nadzab. There we were assigned to quarters (15'X15' pyramidal tents that we would be living in until we headed back to the States). At this time I shared a tent with a fellow by the name of John Schissler.

We were given briefings and then assigned to our first combat mission: two three-plane flights to hit troop concentrations in the Wewak area. Rifkin and I were flying wing in the first flight, Schissler and Rothgeber were flying wing in the second flight. Rifkin developed engine trouble and turned back, so Schissler moved up to his position. When we got to the target, we were supposed to peel off and go in one at a time, strafing and dropping our parademos. I was on the flight leader's left wing (#2 position) so before we peeled off, I had to move over and get on Schissler's wing (that is, we went from a vee formation to an echelon). The flight leader peeled off, then Schissler, then myself. While doing this you had to arm and charge your guns and set up the arming switches for the bomb racks. Then, while on the bomb run itself, you opened the bomb bay doors and prepared to drop.

The bomb bay doors were opened by reaching down with the left hand almost to the floor, grasping a straight handle that came out of the floor and had a button on the end of it, pushing the button in with your thumb, and pushing the handle all of the way down. Several inches above this, on the left side of the cockpit and coming out of the back wall, was the selector valve handle for the landing gear. This handle had a large cube on the end of it. To lower the gear, you grasped the cube, pushed it down to the horizontal position, pulled out on the cube, pushed the lever sideways to negotiate a jog in the downward motion, and then pushed the lever all of the way down. In the excitement of his first combat mission, Schissler actually managed to lower his landing gear instead of opening his bomb bay doors! Of course, his plane slowed down considerably and I came roaring up behind him with all guns blazing. It was lucky that I didn't shoot him down. All this time, every Japanese soldier within shooting distance was blasting away. By the time I caught up to him, he had raised his gear and was accelerating on ahead, so I dropped my bombs and away we went. I hadn't seen anything on the ground except the tracers coming up at me and didn't know whether I hit anything or not. I have to admit, I was absolutely astonished to see that A20 floundering in the air ahead of me with its landing gear hanging down. All of this was a good and sufficient reason for having this sort of introduction to combat flying. If Schissler had done something like that over one of the targets we hit in the Philippines, they would have nailed him for sure.

The first time I saw those tracers coming at me, I had a most peculiar reaction -- one that several others had, as I learned when we talked about it some time later. The reaction was "Why are they shooting at me, I'm a good guy!" A moment later you realize that you are coming in at 300 mph slinging half a ton of .50-cal cartridges and dropping 300-lb bombs on them, not a very friendly act, to say the least.

April 1st was Easter Sunday and I went to the Easter sunrise service. There were about 1400 servicemen present and it was a very moving experience. Then I reported to the flight line and we went on our third mission, but it turned out to be a complete bust. We were scheduled to drop 260-lb fragmentation bombs from medium altitude (3500 feet) by flying in formation with some B25s that we were supposed to meet in the target area. The weather was not good and we had to fly at 6000 feet on top of an overcast to get to the target area. No B25s were anywhere to be seen and we dropped down through a hole in the clouds to about 1000 feet, and still no B25s. We could not drop at low level because the bombs did not have delayed fuses. After half an hour of flubbing around, the leader decided to head back. By this time, the cumulus clouds along the coast were rapidly building and we had to go inland across the mountains to get back to Nadzab. We had to salvo our bombs to get over the mountains because of the building cumulus. I never did find out what happened to the B25s. Maybe they got lost!

That same afternoon, one of our colleagues by the name of Cave was on a local formation flight from Nadzab and had an engine catch on fire. His gunner bailed out, but the wing came off while he was still in the cockpit and he spun in and was killed. In an A20 the main wing spar was directly behind the engine firewall and was very quickly weakened from an engine fire. I wrote a note in my logbook to myself that read: "Moral -- don't fool around with engine fires, bail out!" The accident occurred several miles up river from the air base and the gunner could been seen coming down in his parachute. He survived but it took the rescue party three days to find their way to him in the jungle.

The next day, April 2nd, we had a rerun of our April 1st mission and it was successful. We met the B25s as planned and dropped our bombs from 3500 feet when the lead bombardier toggled off. Then we peeled off and made several strafing runs on many huts along the river.

The air strip at Nadzab consisted of steel segments linked together and laid out on the ground. It was better than operating on dirt, but gave one a sense of insecurity. It rattled as you traversed it and just didn't seem very substantial. Moreover, in some situations it was downright dangerous. In the event of a collapsed nose wheel, the airplane was likely to dig into the mat and roll up like a ball, taking the mat with it. This did happen to one A20 and it rolled into a ball and exploded. Of course, no one got out of it.

There was a squadron of Australians flying B24s at Nadzab that had some really weird missions. They flew their planes almost like fighters, peeling off in steep banks and coming in like they were in P51s. They would take off singly in the evening for long, all-night missions over Japanese positions in Borneo and environs. They would pull up on the end of the steel mat with their tails sticking out over the end of the mat, rev up the engines, and release the brakes. You would see the plane gradually pick up speed and lumber down the runway. Finally, at the last second at the other end of the runway, they would haul back on the control column and force the plane into the air. They would be gone for 17 hours; they must have had fuel packed in every possible place they could. We suspected the crew carried hip flasks full of aviation fuel. They would reach a target area and just fly around dropping a bomb every once in a while to keep the Japanese on alert all night long. Fortunately, the Japanese didn't have any night fighters or they would have been sitting ducks.

One of the experiences we had at Nadzab was to be taken out into the jungle by an Australian trooper for survival training in the jungle. He showed us many interesting things, including what to eat and what not to eat if you were shot down and trying to stay alive. One thing that was really good was what he called "millionaire's celery." If you cut down a palm tree and cut off about 12 to 14" of the growing end, you have something like a stalk of celery, crunchy and with a delicious nutty flavor. Unfortunately, you had to cut down the tree to get it, but it is nourishing and tastes very good. He taught us the proper way to obtain, open, and use coconuts. You drink the milk from a green coconut but don't eat the meat. You eat the meat from a ripe coconut but don't drink the milk because it will lead to diarrhea. We also learned to find passion fruit and a few other more exotic fruits. I wouldn't try the fat, white grubs about an inch long that you find under the bark of decaying trees on the ground. I would have to be in really desperate straits to include them in my menu, but at least I knew how to find them if need be.

While in the jungle, we observed a large spider web with a beautiful, large, black and orange spider clinging to it. The legs must have been eight inches across and the body about two inches long. It was probably a female and had almost a hundred tiny replicas no bigger than a pencil eraser head crawling over and around it. It was a fascinating sight.

When we got back to camp, we had one more lesson from the Aussie about survival in that climate. He told us to be sure to keep as dry as possible under the arms, on the feet, and in the crotch, using baby powder liberally. He made some comment to the effect that it was ridiculous for a grown man like him to be using baby powder, but that it was really important under those conditions. Fungus infections were prevalent, especially among those not native to the area. That was true for Americans of all ethnic backgrounds and the Japanese as well.

8

Liberation of the Philippines

MacArthur Returns

At this point in the Pacific war, MacArthur had returned to the Philippine Islands and "waded ashore" at the time of the landings on Leyte (October 20, 1944). After the fierce naval battle of Leyte Gulf, the Japanese Navy was all but wiped out. They had lost four carriers, three battleships, six cruisers, and twelve destroyers, in addition to hundreds of planes. The Americans had lost a light carrier, two escort carriers, and three destroyers along with less than 200 aircraft.

Ground fighting on Leyte was fierce with many losses on both sides. By the end of December, MacArthur asserted that the Leyte-Samar campaign was over and that all that remained to be done was the "mopping up." The U.S. Eighth army was brought in for the task and fought for another four months, suffering an additional one thousand deaths in what has been described as bitter and rugged fighting. During the whole campaign, the Americans had about four thousand dead, the Japanese almost 60,000. It became clear that enemy resistance became fiercer and more determined the closer we got to Japan, a lesson that was very much in the minds of those planning the invasion of Luzon, the major objective, in January 1945.

General Tomoyuki Yamashita, the conqueror of Malaya, had arrived in Manila in October 1944 to head the Fourteenth Army in the defense of Luzon. By January he still had more than a quarter million troops with ample supplies and ammunition. He planned a defense in depth, instead of using his troops and tanks ineffectively to oppose MacArthur's landings. He concentrated his resources in several defensible positions inland with the goal of encircling the Americans and crushing their forces.

A vast array of over a thousand ships landed some fifty thousand U.S. troops on the northwest coast of Luzon on January 8th, with very little opposition. By the 12th the beachhead at Lingayen gulf was firmly established and the U.S. troops were moving eastward toward the main Japanese defenses in the mountainous areas north-northeast of Lingayen, where Yamashita had his headquarters at Baguio.

East of Lingayen, midway between the towns of Dagupan and Mangaldan, was a series of dry rice paddies where the engineers began moving equipment in on January 17th, grading, compacting, and treating the soil with oil to provide a dirt strip. It was ready for fighters by the 22nd and by the end of the month for light bombers. On the 11th of February, the 312th Bomb Group moved in with their A20s. Previously stationed at Tanuan on Mindoro, they had been flying missions to Luzon since the beginning of the year. The biggest event was the raid on Clark Field on January 7th when the 312th joined with the 417th A20s and 345th B25s in a combined low-level strike. Quoting Lt. Tom Jones of the 389th Squadron, "There were 132 planes in that formation and it was awesome!" As they left Mindoro, the invasion fleet headed for Lingayen Gulf was stretched out before them for miles and miles.

Luzon (Mangaldan airstrip)

Back in New Guinea, I received orders to report with my crew to the 312th Bomb Group on Luzon. We packed our gear and on April 7th hitched rides on Army Air Force transports, staying overnight at Biak, Morotai, and Leyte. We landed at Lingayen air strip and hitched a ride on a truck to 312th Headquarters, located at a dirt strip near Mangaldan. We were assigned to the 387th Squadron. I was assigned to a tent and was surprised to discover that I shared it with John Schissler who had arrived a few days before. I learned later that my friends Rifkin and Blue went to the 417th Bomb Group, Harris and Owens to the 3rd Bomb Group (formerly known as the 3rd Attack). We had all been instructors together at La Junta.

At this point, contact with my gunners, Lawrence and Harris, was drastically reduced. In New Guinea, both of them flew with me on the four combat missions as well as several training missions. In the 312th, all gunners were put into a pool. Since only one gunner was assigned to a plane on each mission, the gunners flew only half as often as the pilots. This was difficult for them because it meant that it would take them twice as long to accumulate enough points for rotation back to the States as it took the pilots. Moreover, it was unlikely that you would draw one of your own gunners on any given mission.

Another aspect of being a replacement pilot at this point in the war is that none of us had planes assigned to us permanently. Instead, plane assignments were made at the time missions were scheduled. Since I kept track of which planes I flew on each mission, I was able to summarize my experiences in this way: in 43 A20 missions, I flew 24 different airplanes, 13 of them only once, and very seldom the same plane twice in a row. One of the planes I flew most frequently was an A20G marked with a large plus "+" on the vertical stabilizer instead of a letter.

Major Miller was Squadron commander in the 387th and Capt. Tranchitella the operations officer. I had an orientation flight in the Group B25J on the 12th and flew my first A20 mission with the 387th on the 20th. In the meantime, the group had moved from the airstrip up at Lingayen, to a small dirt strip near the town of Floridablanca, about ten miles south of Clark Field, the main AAF base in the area. The nearest major town was Angeles, just a few miles away. The runway was short (5000 ft) with a small hill at one end of it, so we could only take off in one direction and land in the opposite direction. (Things as messed up as that must have taken a great deal of operational planning at headquarters. I guess that's why there were so many high-ranking officers on the headquarters staff...) The good news was that the engineers were hard at work on a new 7000-foot all-weather strip for us.

Floridablanca

On arrival at Floridablanca, Schissler and I had to put up our own tent. It was quite a job and took us a good part of the day. (Tent erection had not been one of the subjects covered in Ground School.) The bivouac area was set out on a flat piece of treeless land edged on one side by an embankment with a steep drop of 15-20 feet to a small wooded region. A dirt road led off about half a mile or a mile to the airstrip.

Sanitary facilities were primitive but adequate. Latrines were out in the open and consisted only of rectangular wooden boxes containing four "seats"; each box covered a septic trench in the ground. The shower area was also open and consisted only of a floor with overhead pipes from which the water flowed. It took me several days before I became accustomed to talking to the girls delivering or picking up laundry while I was sitting on the latrine box or taking a shower. We had a mess tent with picnic-style tables for eating. The enlisted men had a larger bivouac area but essentially the same kind of facilities.

We slept on standard army cots, but had mosquito netting hanging from above and tucked in around us at night. Malaria was quite prevalent in the area and there were lots of mosquitos. We took atabrine tablets daily to ward off symptoms of malaria; the tablets gave everyone's skin a yellowish hue. The nights were warm and muggy. I found that frequently I had my bare knee up against the netting and would have several mosquito bites on it in the morning. Another thing that was most unsettling was that rats would frequently make their way into the tent at night and you could hear them chewing on the plastic buttons on our raincoats. I can't imagine there was much nutrition in them... Anyway, one of us would throw something and they would go away for a while. One night I woke up in a panic with my heart pounding; it felt like a rat had run across my chest. It couldn't have happened because my mosquito netting was well tucked in, but it gave me a start, nevertheless.

My first mission with the 312th was rather uneventful until we got back to the base. There was the familiar greeting, "Report to the C.O.'s office!" It seems Major Miller was down at the flight line that morning watching the squadron take off and he didn't like the way I did it. I had a habit of holding the plane low on the runway until I had retracted the landing gear and then climbing out as the airspeed picked up. The A20 had a bit more of a tendency to settle as the gear came up than the B25 did and he thought I should start my climb sooner. I was the only one in the squadron that had as much flying time as he did, but I didn't argue the point. He was a major and the squadron commander. I was still a second lieutenant. Next day he had me watch the rest of the squadron take off on that day's mission.

This brings up the subject of promotion. The myth going around was that promotions came fast in the Air Corps. That certainly was not true in the training command. None of the guys with me from the class of 43-J had been promoted yet, although at this point we had been second lieutenants for almost a year and a half. When we got into our groups overseas, they were amazed that we were still second looies and put us all in for promotion. Mine came through on July 1st; Ed Kent and John Schissler were on the same set of orders.

My sixth mission (April 22) was at medium altitude; we had 500-lb bombs containing a newer explosive called RDX. Since the new explosive was more powerful and more sensitive to shock than the standard TNT, we couldn't drop them from low altitude. A premature burst at low altitude would certainly destroy the plane as well. We flew formation on the Group B25 and dropped from 3000 ft when the bombardier in the B25 released his. The target was an ammunition dump at Pattao. All bombs landed in the target area and we observed heavy explosions and much smoke. At 3000 ft we could actually hear the bombs detonating and feel the shock waves.

Although the Japanese troops had been pushed out of the villages and valleys, many of them were holed up in the hills. They came down at night to raid the air bases and steal food. One of the few diversions we had at night were the movies, shown on an outdoor screen. Many nights during this period the movie was stopped and canceled when there were alerts from the Philippine guards that Japanese were infiltrating the area and small arms fire would be heard. The night of April 22nd was a particularly bad one. About 20 Japanese soldiers were killed on the field and in town. My former gunner, Leroy Harris, was in town and had a hand in shooting one of them. Although they were not a significant military threat, they were still a serious threat because of their military code -- no surrender. I slept that night with my .45-cal pistol at my head. Just two weeks later, two Japanese soldiers were discovered one morning by one of our pilots on the other side of the embankment, about 100 yards from our tent. He fired at them; fearing capture, they blew themselves up with a grenade. What a bloody mess!

April 26th would have been my eighth mission but I had to drop out. The hydraulic strut on my left landing gear collapsed and it wouldn't retract into the wheel well. Since bombs were in short supply, we had been ordered not to salvo them (i.e., drop them unarmed) unless it was absolutely necessary. So, I had to return to the field with a full load of fuel, bombs, and ammunition. With the tall hill at one end of the strip, I had to land with a slight tail wind. When I reached the end of the runway, I was still doing about 60 mph and not about to stop. Fortunately, the ground was hard and dry and I was able to continue across the road at the end of the strip and come to a stop a few hundred yards on the other side. (Luckily, there were no ditches on either side of the road.) As I was rolling across the road, I noticed a truck stopped on the road and the driver staring at me with his mouth hanging open. He was as surprised as I was!

My old buddy finally caught up to me on the 30th. Ed Kent came walking into the tent. He had finished at the CRTC, was sent to the 312th Bomb Group, assigned to the 387th Squadron, and then assigned to the tent with Schissler and me. It was quite remarkable and we were happy to see each other again. I didn't realize it at the time, but a week later discovered that it was one of the luckiest things ever to happen to me. Shortly after he arrived in the group, they received orders to transfer the latest pilot to join the group to the 345th Bomb Group at Clark Field as a B25 copilot. It was Ed Kent, and if he hadn't been there it would have been Robert Hornbeck. I hated to see Ed go, but felt very deeply, better him than me! At that point we had been together 2 years and 1 month, practically a lifetime in wartime service. I noted in my logbook that he was on his way to be a hydraulic engineer and wheel-jerker. Our old friend Bufkin had gone to the 3rd Bomb Group on Mindoro.

Some time later I learned that Ed's plane had been shot down coming back from a B25 strike on Formosa. He bailed out and was in his one-man life raft in the water when a submarine surfaced nearby. He was so groggy from the parachute drop that he began fumbling to get his pistol out of his shoulder holster, thinking it was a Japanese sub. Fortunately, it was an American boat and he was rescued by them. I don't know if he flew any more missions, but he did get back home to his wife and daughter in Southern California.

On my ninth mission, April 28th, my plane received its first hit as far forward as the pilot's compartment. A .25-cal slug hit the side of the fuselage just 12-14" below the seat and stopped inside the wheel well. Fortunately, it did not hit the nose wheel itself so I didn't have a flat nose wheel when I landed. This can be a severe problem when landing on a dirt strip because the nose wheel strut can collapse and the plane can flip over. We rarely got hits as far forward as the pilot's compartment because of the speed we flew on our low-level attacks. We would come in at 280-300 mph and have very few hits, while the B25s would come in on the same targets at 240-250 mph and really get shot up. I guess the Japanese gunners just didn't "lead" us enough, but they were well zeroed in on the B25s.

I also noted on that mission that I observed the 50-foot pole that the Japs used to string cable across potential flight paths. They tried various means to bring down planes or hamper attacks. In addition to stringing cables, they would sometimes detonate mines in the tops of trees, trying to catch a low-flying plane in the blast or in the debris. At 300 mph we were moving over the treetops at 440 feet per second, so it wasn't easy. Later, in June, we noticed large black cylindrical objects lobbed into the air like mortar shells. They were obviously trying to hit planes with them; one gunner said that he saw one explode, but we never did figure out what they were. In time, three of our planes were hit by them but they did not explode when they hit and did little damage. Perhaps they were mortar shells with short fuses, but that could present problems to the people on the ground, too. Flying that low, they could even throw rocks at us.

One of the things we enjoyed doing when the target was limited in size and there was a lot of flat ground around it was to exercise our opportunity for flying "on the deck." Once away from the target, we sometimes had a chance to fly as low and as fast as we could, hopping over fences, chasing water buffalo, horses, or whatever, until it was necessary to join up in formation again for the flight home. I guess it helped work off some of the adrenalin that had pumped into your system on the strafing run.

A flight to Tanuan on May 3rd in our Group B25 was what we called a "fat-cat." This was slang for a courier flight to an air base not currently in a combat zone for the purpose of carrying military communications, picking up supplies, etc. Whenever we could, we took advantage of the opportunity to visit the quartermaster warehouses to buy personal items like clothing, sheets, etc. which were not furnished to officers through squadron supply. On the other hand, I was unhappy about missing out on both of the missions flown by the group that day

A popular item on such a trip was to stock up on Tee-shirts and khaki trousers. These were great for bartering with our local fresh egg and fruit vendors. One time we were able to barter a pair of khaki trousers for 54 fresh eggs. We hard-boiled them all and invited all our friends in the area in to share in the largess. Other popular items were bananas and mangoes.

One pleasant surprise I had on joining the 312th Bomb Group was to discover that several of the students that we had trained at La Junta had gone into A20s and were in the group. One of them was Phillips, one of my students from my first class, 44-C. He was on the May 5th mission with me to Solano (my 11th) and had a quite dramatic experience. He was flying "T," the oldest A20 in the

SWPA; it had over 600 combat hours and still retained its original engines. His right engine started trailing smoke just after coming off the target, probably from a hit on an oil line. The engine cut out once or twice and our flight leader, "Red" Cleveland left the formation to take him to Lingayen, which was much closer than our base. Upon reaching Lingayen, the engine burst into flames, so he and the gunner bailed out. They both landed near the airstrip, only 300 yards from where the plane crashed. One of the less desirable aspects of the A20 that we didn't dwell on was that it was a very difficult plane for the pilot to bail out of without injury. The pilot sat forward of the propellers and there was a clearance of only six inches between the propeller tips and the side of the fuselage. It was critically important for the pilot to get out on the wing and roll off of the trailing edge, but that had to be done in such a way as to avoid being hit by the horizontal stabilizer. If the plane were flying straight and level on autopilot (which we didn't have) it might have been possible, but in a plane out of control it was virtually impossible. Consequently, Phillips fractured his leg when it hit the horizontal stabilizer and was not in very good shape when his parachute landed. He came out of it OK and was rotated back to the States, but we were anxious about him for a while. The gunner had no difficulty and was soon back on duty. Ironically, it was his first mission.

On April 30th one of our students from La Junta (class of 44-E) by the name of Ralph C. Smith was killed when he crashed on take-off. A few weeks later two others from the same class, Omar S. Potts and Robert E. Simms, were killed when their planes collided while joining up in formation after take-off. The gunner in one of the planes survived by jumping out of the tunnel hatch while the fuselage was sliding along the ground on its side. He said he thought he was going to be killed anyway and decided to take a chance on jumping out. He was one lucky guy!

Not long after that another student from 44-E by the name of Overholzer, who was in the 417th Bomb Group, was killed when his plane went down over the target. Although still stationed on Mindoro, the 417th came up to Luzon to hit some of the same targets that we did. His flight was too close to the lead flight going over the target and was caught in their bomb blasts. His two wing men each had their inboard engines knocked out by the blasts but both were able to limp into Clark Field on one engine. I saw one of the planes and it was really shot up, about 200 holes.

We frequently carried five racks of 23-pound fragmentation bombs in our bomb bay for missions against Japanese troops both in exposed and forested conditions. Each rack contained sixteen bombs, for a total of eighty. The bombs were released one at a time, one-third of a second apart. At 300 mph, this would be a bomb every fifty yards. Flying three planes abreast, it was possible to cover a fairly large area. The bombs were armed when they hit the slipstream and the parachutes were pulled out. They were detonated by large tee-shaped fuses on the nose that would go off on striking even a limb of a tree. In such an attack, it was critically important not to follow too closely behind the flight ahead of you to avoid being caught in their bomb blasts. That was what happened to Overholzer's flight.

On May 8th we received word that the war in Europe was over. I made an entry in my logbook to the effect that we had finished England's war and now we could go to work and finish our own. In retrospect, a rather jingoistic statement, but it reflected how most of us out in the Pacific felt about the war in Europe. It was patently obvious that, until then, most of the U.S. effort was going to the war in Europe. With the advantage today of 20/20 hindsight, that policy appears to have been completely justifiable.

South China Sea

Progress on the Ground

During this period, the central plain south of Lingayen had been cleared out, Manila Bay cleared, and after much fighting, the city of Manila had been liberated. The American 25th Division had advanced along Route 5 and was approaching Balete Pass, but with stiffening resistance as they fought their way up to the thirty-five-hundred-foot pass. This pass led over into the Cagayan Valley which was still controlled by very strong Japanese forces. Many of our missions in the following days were in support of the troops fighting their way up Highway 5, which traveled through Balete Pass, into the Cagayan Valley and to Tuguegarao, a provincial capital; however, severe fighting was still going on in the "watershed" area southeast of Manila and we ran several ground-support missions in that area, as well.

On my 14th mission, May 10th, we used our new, 7000-foot, hard-surface, all-weather strip at Floridablanca that the engineers had been working on for a couple of months. It was such a pleasure to use, compared to the old dirt strip (especially after the exciting landing I had made on April 26th). During dry spells the dirt strip was miserable for take-offs when going on missions. With all the planes taxiing out, the dust was so thick that sometimes we could see only the vertical stabilizer of the plane ahead of us. We had to taxi with the windows closed and the hot tropical sun pouring in through the Plexiglass made the cockpit like an oven. By the time we got in the air, we were wrung out from the heat.

May 11th saw the first use of wing-mounted napalm bombs. These were 100-lb bombs fastened to our wing racks in clusters of three and on many of our subsequent missions we carried one cluster on each wing rack. Demolition bombs were usually carried in the bomb bay and were retarded by parachutes that deployed when the bomb was released. Occasionally a parachute would tear off of a bomb when it came out of the bomb bay and hit the slipstream. The bomb would stay close to the plane and could bounce back almost to the altitude of the plane. This was caught on one of our rear-facing cameras. For obvious reasons, parachute-retarded bombs could only be carried in the bomb bay and had 3-4 second delay fuses. Bombs which were not parachute-retarded were carried on the wing racks and had 8-15 second delay fuses.

May 16th was my sixteenth mission, a low-level strafing and bombing attack on the town of San Juan, reported to be full of Japanese troops and Japanese "sympathizers." I was rather skeptical of the latter since, for the most part, the Filipinos hated the Japanese troops and there would not have been many civilian sympathizers among them.

On May 23rd an intelligence bulletin was posted stating that our mission to San Juan on the 16th had been extremely successful. Ground observers reported that 100% of the bombs fell in the target area. Gasoline, ammo, and food dumps were completely destroyed. Over 200 Japanese troops had been killed and the remainder scattered to the hills. Dugouts, gun positions, and equipment were destroyed. The target was reported as being "eliminated." It was encouraging to hear that we were getting good results, even though we couldn't see much evidence of it from the air.

Mission #17, (May 17th): I took off as spare and then took Pritchard's place when he was delayed in his takeoff. We always flew in three-plane elements on missions. On the way to the target and return, we flew in vees of three planes each, staggered down from the leading element. The flight leader in each vee would position himself below and behind the flight leader in the vee ahead of him and the wing men would similarly be placed below and behind the wing men in the forward vee. On reaching the target, the vees would peel off one after the other; the wing men would move forward and level with the flight leader, so the three-plane element would go in "line abreast" to avoid getting caught in the bomb blasts from the adjacent planes. On the return flight, we would form the same configuration we had going out, filling in the vees if someone had dropped out or gone down over the target. In order to maintain the integrity of the three-plane elements, we usually had a "spare," a fully equipped plane and a crew briefed on the mission that took off with the rest of the group. If someone was unable to get off the ground and take his assigned place in the formation, or dropped out while the group was forming up, the spare would take his place. If all planes made it into the formation, the spare would land and stand down from the mission.

On that particular day, I was assigned the function of spare. When Pritchard started an engine, his wing bombs dropped on the ground; somewhat disconcerting, to say the least. Of course, they were not armed and no damage was done, so he shut off his engine and they mounted the bombs back on the racks. In the meantime, flying alongside the assembling formation, I was told to take his place on Eddie Bretch's wing, which I did. While the formation was still assembling, Pritchard caught up to us and signaled for me to move out of his position. Not wanting planes to be changing places in the formation at that point, which is always a dangerous operation, Bretch signaled me to stay put, and I was only too happy to do so. When I got back to base, Pritchard raised hell with me for cutting him out on the mission; I gave him back in kind since what I had done was supported by the flight leader.

This matter of changing positions in a formation reminds me of one of the things that I looked forward to the least. On returning to base after a mission, the three-plane vees would go to three-plane echelons to the right. In this way, each flight leader would peel off for landing first, then the right wing man, and finally the left wing man who was now flying in the rightmost position. The worst place to be in this maneuver was left wing man (#2 position) on one of the lower elements. On signal, it was necessary to raise up sufficiently to clear both the flight leader's plane and the right wing man (#3 position), slide across to the right, and then lower yourself into position on #3's right wing. On the crossover, you were flying directly in the prop wash of the three planes in the element ahead of you and you were fighting the controls all of the way, while trying desperately not to collide with the two planes directly below you. It was a dangerous and frustrating maneuver, but it sure looked great from the ground, and that's what the C.O. wanted. For some reason or other, I almost always found myself assigned to that unfortunate position (Tail-end-Charlie!).

Mission #19, on May 25th, was our first close ground support attack against fortified troops that was coordinated with fighters dropping napalm. P38s and P51s went in with two 110-gal tanks of napalm each, causing the enemy troops to leap out of their foxholes and dugouts to escape the liquid fire pouring down into them. This exposed them to attack by the A20s and automatic weapons fire from the U.S. troops. We were told that these attacks were so successful that our ground troops could walk right in on fortified areas that had previously kept them pinned down, unable to advance.

Frequently on close ground support missions, I would look down and see the GIs in their foxholes as I passed less than 50 feet above them. The soldiers in the forward foxholes would place a red smoke grenade on the edge of the foxhole and anything beyond that was "target." At moments like that, I was happy to be up where I was and not down there in a hole in the ground. I really felt a sense of responsibility to do what I could to help those guys survive.

One day while I was preparing to go on a practice formation and skip-bombing hop with the squadron, I had a long, lanky infantry sergeant approach me and ask if he could go along for the ride, which was something he had wanted to do for a long time. He wanted to ride up front, where he could see what was going on, not in the gunner's position in the rear. So, I opened the canopy and tossed out the life raft to make room for him in the piggyback position, got him a parachute, and briefed him on the flight. We went out to Subic Bay and "dusted off" some of the Navy ships. It was great sport to fly along at 300+ mph skimming the water, waving to the sailors looking down on us from up on their decks. We flew so low we could actually see a wake in the water from our prop wash. When we got back and landed, the sergeant unwrapped himself from his cramped position, got on the ground, and said, "Lieutenant, you're a little guy but you sure know how to handle that plane!" That more than paid for his ride.

Mission #22 to Santiago on May 29th was noteworthy for two reasons: for the first time on a combat mission I was flying an "H" model, with the more powerful engines and what a joy it was to have that added power! The second reason has to do with the civilians I saw in the target area. I came in on my strafing run and set up the switches to arm the racks for dropping the 23-lb parafrags; I reached down to open my bomb bay doors. I was flying at about 50 feet going right down the side of a hedgerow, and noticed something I had never seen before. Lying side-by-side on their stomachs, in a row, with heads against the hedgerow and arms over their heads for protection, were 35-40 civilians from the town.

I passed directly over them and could see them very clearly. I hoped that I hadn't hit any of them with my strafing and made sure that I didn't toggle off any parafrags until I was well past them, but it bothered me nonetheless. We were frequently told in intelligence briefings not to worry about civilians in the target area because they were probably Japanese sympathizers and collaborators, but I think that was said to ease our consciences. Not very many Filipinos were sympathetic to the Japanese. I couldn't help but feel there were some innocent civilians down there. Even today, 57 years later, the scene is vivid in my memory. In today's parlance such casualties are euphemistically referred to as "collateral damage." It is an indictment of civilization that killing civilians can be viewed so cavalierly.

Consolidated B32 Dominator in the 386th Squadron

Arrival of the B32 Dominators

The end of May saw a significant change in the character of the 312th Bomb Group. Consolidated Aircraft B32s were brought in and the 386th Squadron was converted to Very Heavy Bombardment. The B32 was Consolidated's counterpart to the Boeing B29 Superfortress and was meant to provide a backup for the B29 program in case it was delayed. It was a four-engine high-altitude bomber with greater range, bomb load, and firepower than the B29, but it arrived much later in the war. The 312th Bomb Group had been chosen as the outfit to introduce these planes into combat. The A20 pilots, gunners, and planes of the 386th were divided between the 388th and 389th Squadrons. None went to the 387th because it was next on the list to convert to B32s.

June was a busy month; by the 24th I had flown 18 combat missions, been on several practice flights, checked out in the Group C47 and flew four courier flights to Mindoro. On one of the courier flights, I saw Bufkin and learned that his group was changing to Douglas A26s, the "big brother" to the A20. No monstrous B32s for them! The A26 (Invader) was a powerful, low-level attack plane. It had 2200-hp Pratt & Whitney engines and a fuselage wide enough for side-by-side seating. However, the right hand seat was for a flight engineer and not a copilot. Although there were flight controls on the right side, the plane could not be flown from there, as a B25 could. It could carry a considerably heavier bomb load than the A20 and, in some versions, had as many as 14 forward-firing .50-cal machine guns (eight in the nose and three on each wing. It also had two remotely-controlled turrets with twin .50-cal guns. However, it had one serious defect for low-level missions: the massive engine nacelles protruded so far forward of the pilot that you could not see planes alongside of you. When the 7th Air Force first tried low-level missions in these planes, they lost several of them by running into each other on the deck because the pilots couldn't keep track of the planes adjacent to them. In spite of that, it was an excellent plane and I had the opportunity to check out in it and fly it after the war. It played a big part in the Korean war when it was re-designated as the B26. The original B26, the Martin Marauder, was deactivated when WWII ended.

June 6th (the first anniversary of D-day for the Normandy invasion), was a bad one. We had a P51 wing operating out of the same airstrip with us. As we were taxiing out to take off in the morning, one of the P51s crashed on take off, right at the end of the runway. He was carrying 500-lb bombs and we had to wait for 45 minutes while the plane burned. Finally, we taxied 3/4ths of the way down the runway and took off short in the opposite direction. One of the bombs went off after we took off. I was also on a mission in the afternoon. Biederman, of the 389th Squadron, was joining formation, reefed back the control column too hard, and hit a high-speed stall. His plane crashed and burned immediately. Neither he nor his gunner got out.

On the 10th, after I came back from the morning mission and was riding a Jeep back to the ready room, there was an explosion and fire on the flight line. Two planes of the 389th caught fire while being refueled. The fire and explosions were spectacular. No one was injured but the planes were total losses.

On July 4th the 387th Squadron was broken up and I was assigned to the 388th. Rumors were many and wild about what would happen to the remaining A20 squadrons. My friend Britton and I went up to Lingayen on the 5th to see about getting into night fighters. Col. O'Dell, the C.O. of the P61 squadron there, said they were expecting some new crews in but if they didn't show up, he would need pilots badly. In that event, he said he would be happy to check us out in P61s and put us in his squadron. Hope springs eternal; there was still a remote possibility of getting into P61s, and I hadn't given up, yet. However, it turned out to be more "remote" than "possible."

Pilots of the 387th Bomb Squadron (Floridablanca, Luzon, July 2,1945)

We received word on the 12th that the 388th and 389th were going up to Okinawa with 16 A20s each. We started a series of intelligence lectures on Kyushu, our new target area. It gradually became clear to us that the powers-that-be had written off the A20 units as expendable and were sending us up for some rugged missions with great potential for heavy losses. We were going to be hitting port facilities, coming in across the water to harass the shore installations while medium and heavy bombers were hitting inland. The targets were described as having three hundred fifty to four hundred 90-mm AA guns along the harbor. All they had to do was set up a barrage in the water so that we would have to fly through it on the deck. In addition, the missions were at our maximum range. The briefer advised us that turning the wrong way coming off the target might mean insufficient fuel to make it back. They had planned for U.S. subs to be stationed at various places to and from the target for A20s to ditch, if necessary. I remembered ditching drill for the A20 at Charlotte; they had a fuselage set up and we had to practice getting out of the seat, throwing the life raft off the wing, and jumping into the water (but we didn't actually do it in water). They said at the time that the A20 was supposed to float for 50 seconds after landing on the water, but not to count on more than 10! Thanks, but no thanks. Most of us felt that higher command considered the two A20 squadrons expendable and were just going to use us while we lasted. We were not optimistic about our prospects.

After my 42nd mission (Floridablanca)

On July 20th I flew my last combat strike in an A20. This mission was a first for us because we flew ground support with Filipino guerrilla troops in the mountains. The guerrillas were doing most of the mopping up operations at this point; our own troops were preparing for the coming invasion of Japan.

On August 7th, we received word of the atomic bomb dropped on Hiroshima. Then, the second one on Nagasaki on the 9th. Also on the 9th, Russia declared war on Japan. At this point, the 386th and 387th Squadrons were loaded on LSTs in Subic Bay, waiting to move up to Okinawa. Headquarters personnel were already on Okinawa preparing to set up operations. Everything was packed for the 388th and 389th Squadrons, and we were waiting for the move. One more important item had to be taken care of. On August 15th, my friend Schissler and I took off in the group C47 for Okinawa, bearing a precious load. We were carrying the lumber to rebuild the 312th Bomb Group Officers' Club! That would make the move final, irrevocable, and official.

We were off the ground at 0815 and at 0830 I tuned in WVTM on the radio compass. We heard the announcement that the war was over. After an uneventful trip, we arrived at Okinawa about 1500. Schissler went to look up his brother in a nearby Marine Corps outfit and I went over to look up Bufkin in the 3rd Bomb Group, whose area was next to ours. I recorded in my logbook that I saw Buff, Owens, Rocky Haines, Poe, Morganelli, and Major Fredericks. At this time, I can only recall Buff and Poe -- the same Poe who was in my first class of students at La Junta. We had a wild celebration that night, although I learned it was tame compared to the one they had several nights before when the word spread prematurely that the war was over. At that time, there was much shooting into the air, everything from pistols to antiaircraft guns, and I heard that several men were wounded from the bullets and shell fragments falling from the sky. I thought of this recently when the Kuwaitis and others were wildly firing automatic weapons into the air when their country was liberated. The law of gravity hasn't been repealed -- what goes up must still come down (unless it has reached escape velocity, of course). The next day we had a nice flight back in good weather. Since the war was still on when we took off the previous morning and were flying into a combat zone; we got credit for combat time on the 15th, so it was recorded as my 44th mission.

Last Aerial Combat of the War

Although hostilities officially ended on August 15th, B32s of the 386th Squadron had not seen the end of enemy action. Photo reconnaissance missions were flown over Tokyo on the 17th and 18th to locate suitable airfields for airborne troops who were to precede the occupation troops. Although the B32s were equipped with cameras, we did not have any aerial photographers in the Group for such a photo-recon mission so two photographers were borrowed from the 20th Long Range Reconnaissance Squadron. Various accounts differ on the exact dates for these two events but I will present a version consistent with the official records.

On August 17th four B32s flying over Tokyo on a reconnaissance mission were attacked by approximately ten Japanese fighters. B32 gunners warded off the attacks and claimed two enemy fighters shot down, but there was no confirmation and they may not have actually succeeded in downing them, The next day, four B32s again were attacked over Tokyo, this time by fourteen fighters in a running battle that continued for about twenty minutes. On this occasion, gunners of the B32 piloted by Lt. John B. Anderson did down two fighters and the crew received official credit in a communique issued by Headquarters Fifth Air Force on October 10, 1945. However, two photographers on detached duty from the 20th Reconnaissance Squadron were on board. One of them, Sgt. Anthony Marchione, was killed and the other, Sgt. Joseph Lacharite, was wounded. One engine was damaged and Lt. Anderson had to fly home on three engines.

I have a website dedicated to the 312th Bomb Group at: rfhornbeck.home.attbi.com (which has many more pictures from that time). One day I received an e-mail from a young Japanese man by the name of Yasuyoshi Kitano. His wife Magda is a granddaughter of Joe Lacharite and he had been researching the events of August 17 and 18, 1945. Interestingly, he had interviewed some of the Japanese pilots who had attacked the B32s. With respect to dating the events, he ran into the same difficulty, with different dates given by different interviewees. The most astonishing thing was that Japan's greatest surviving ace, Saburo Sakai, led one of the attacks. Sakai described how, not knowing these were reconnaissance flights and mindful of the atom bomb attacks on Hiroshima and Nagasaki, the fighter pilots rushed to their planes to engage the enemy with all possible speed, thinking that perhaps the U.S. bombers were abrogating the cease-fire.

August 28th saw the last two missions before the official end of the war. At 0545 two B32s were preparing to take off on a communications mission over Atsugi and Tokyo. As one of them took off, it lost power on one engine and hurtled over the cliff at the end of the runway and exploded in a ball of fire. All thirteen crew members died instantly.

At 0730 on the same day, three B32s took off for what was to be a fourteen hour mission over Tokyo. On return, after eleven hours in the air, one of the planes had trouble with two engines that had to be shut down. Unable to maintain altitude on the other two engines, the pilot (2nd Lt. Collins Orton) gave the order to bail out about 175 miles north of Okinawa.. All thirteen crew members got out; fortunately, some U.S. destroyers in the area were able to save twelve of them but Cpl. Morris Morgan was never found. In addition, after being rescued, S/Sgt George Murphy died from injuries received.

Early in September I was included in a group of 312th Bomb Group pilots (I believe there were 14 of us) taken down to Biak, New Guinea in the Group C47 to ferry some new A20Hs up to the Philippines. We had a couple of local shake-down flights in the Biak area to make sure the planes were operating O.K. and on September 10th started the first leg of our trip to Morotai, in the Halmaheras. It was about 600 miles over the open sea and, near the midpoint, we crossed the equator. Arrival at Morotai was uneventful and we stayed overnight. At this time, only the airstrip and the surrounding environs were in Allied hands; the rest of the island was still held by the Japanese, most of whom did not yet recognize that the war was over.

The next morning we took off and headed for Zamboanga, on the southwest tip of Mindanao (also approximately 600 miles). Again we arrived without incident and proceeded to land. As I was taxiing in, I had the strange feeling that the ground surface was somehow moving. On shutting down the engines and climbing out of the plane, I discovered why. The entire surface was covered with a moving mass of locusts, all about the same color as the ground they covered. It was almost impossible to avoid stepping on them and it was a messy business indeed. We gassed up and headed on the last leg of the journey, about 500 miles to Clark Field, Luzon. Flying over the seas around the Philippine Islands gave us a picture of the massive naval forces in the area, with ships spread out in every direction almost as far as the eye could see. We landed at Clark Field, parked the A20s with many hundreds of other new combat planes (B17s, B24s, B25s, P51s, etc.) and headed back to our unit. It was ironic that all of these new combat planes were arriving now that the war was over; we would have been so happy to have them just a few months before.

On September 24th we received word that the 312th Bomb Group was deactivated. All of our planes were taken down to Biak; personnel with over 100 hours of combat time or more than eight months overseas were to be returned to the States. Pilots not meeting those requirements were assigned to Troop Carrier and sent up to Okinawa. Some of them eventually ended up in Japan. On October 10th, those of us returning to the States moved down to Manila to await final orders.

I don't have any further entries in my logbook and have only dim memories of the trip home. I do remember that when we were assigned to a ship for the voyage home we stood in line with our baggage for twelve hours waiting to board ship. Nobody left that line and nobody complained; we would have waited all night to get on that ship, if necessary. We came sailing into San Francisco harbor on Thanksgiving Day. The sky was overcast and the weather rather dreary, but it sure looked good to us. In large letters, they spelled out on the hills around the harbor "Welcome Home -- Well Done!" It really boosted our morale. We got off the ship at Camp Stoneman that evening and had a great Thanksgiving dinner, the best food any of us had since leaving the States. Unfortunately, it was also the richest, and many of us spent much of the night on the pot because of it. I had gotten down to a bare 135 pounds overseas, the lowest my weight had been since high school. I got home to Chicago on December 8th and almost froze my butt off. All I had to wear were my suntans and a thin field jacket and the mercury was hovering at about 8 above zero. The important things were that the war was over, I had survived, and I was home again.

9

Meteorology School (NYU)

I returned to Illinois Institute of Technology to resume my studies in chemistry in March 1946. I had previously matriculated as a student in chemical engineering, but decided to change my major to chemistry. I had a heavy schedule, 19 semester hours, with organic chemistry, physics, calculus, economics, and German. In the expansion of college training and the onslaught of the GI Bill veterans, teaching staffs were rather hastily augmented. I had a German-speaking physics professor who could barely speak English and an Italian-speaking professor teaching my German class who could barely speak English or German. It was a challenging experience.

In addition to the usual difficulties of adapting to peacetime civilian life, I missed exceedingly being able to fly. I had a good friend who had also become a pilot during the war and we would get together over a few beers to talk about flying and fantasize joining the Nationalist Chinese air force or the Greek air force (also fighting communists at the time), but nothing ever came of it. Although I was doing well enough in my studies, keeping up an "A" average, I would run out of the house to look up when a military plane flew overhead.

I joined the Air Reserve Unit stationed out at Orchard Place Airport, on the northwest side of Chicago and participated in some of the Reserve activities flying AT6s. One memorable occasion was on July 4th, 1947, when I participated in a large formation of AT6s flying over Soldiers Field in an observance of Independence Day.

But — it wasn't enough. In the spring of 1947 I went to the Fifth Army Headquarters in Chicago and talked to a colonel about the possibility of getting back on active duty. He asked me what my primary MOS (Military Occupational Specialty) was and when I replied "Twin-engine pilot," he shook his head and said "No chance." They had more twin-engine pilots on active duty than they knew what to do with, and weren't about to take on any more. Downhearted, I was prepared to leave when he suddenly inquired "Do you have two years of college math?" I answered that I most certainly did (at the time I was finishing up a course in differential equations). He then told me that he could put me on active duty and send me to a university to study meteorology for a year if I would sign an agreement to serve for four years as a weather officer after finishing my training. I replied that my principal reason for going back on active duty was to fly and he assured me that I would continue on flying status and would have to keep up all of the flying requirements in addition to weather duties. That sounded like the best of all possible worlds to me and I immediately applied for the program. I was surprised to learn that the need for weather officers was so severe because they had trained so many of them during the war. However, when the war ended, most of them got out and went back to civilian life. Some of those who had been inclined to stay on active duty realized that non-flying officers would have difficulty competing with flying officers in the postwar air force.

So, on August 24th, 1947, I was called to active duty and proceeded to my assignment at New York University to begin meteorology training. We had a class of 55 reserve officers, not all of whom had aeronautical ratings. In fact, one or two were actually naval officers who had been given commissions in the Army Air Force in order to participate in the program. Actually, on or about September 1, 1947 the War Department and the Navy Department were combined into the Defense Department. The two services were now three separate ones! At the same time, Assistant Secretaries were appointed for the Army, the Navy, and the Air Force, which then operated as separate entities. It was at that time that the Air Force adopted the blue uniforms universally used by them today, but for several years officers were permitted to wear either the new blue uniform or the old army "pinks and greens."

Life at NYU

We lived like civilians, renting rooms in the Bronx, near the Engineering College of NYU, where we had all of our classes. I teamed up with Bob Alter, a captain from Fort Wayne, Indiana. He had been stationed at Pearl Harbor early in the war and had flown the OA10, the army's version of the PBY5 (Catalina flying boat). They would start out before dawn and fly out to the limit of their range, then come in low looking for enemy submarines which might be caught on the surface in the light of the morning sun.

Bob was able to get a room in a neighboring building so that his window was directly opposite mine, which made it convenient for getting together at mealtimes or whenever we were going out together. He had his car with him and several of us would ride out to Mitchel Field with him on weekends to get in our flying time. Ed Hart and Lyle Danke were the other two pilots who went with us and we would get AT6s or B25s or C47s to tool around in for half a day of "local flying." Occasionally, when the opportunity presented itself, Lyle and I would get a B25 and fly to Chicago for a long weekend to get in some navigational time. On one such occasion, we buzzed the neighborhood where I lived and I revved up the props as we flew over at low altitude. It happened just when the sergeant in the local police station was taking role and I understand he was more than a little agitated over the ruckus we made. Fortunately, nobody turned me in.

On one of the B25 flights to Chicago with Lyle Danke, we carried as a passenger a Navy lieutenant commander assigned to the battleship U.S.S. Missouri, which was in port in the New York area. He was so happy to get home to Chicago for a visit that when we returned to Mitchel Field, he invited us to have dinner with him on the Missouri and to show us around the ship. We did so and we had a most enjoyable time. The dinner was far more elaborate than any I had ever had in the army, including silver tea and coffee service, as well as china dinnerware and silver utensils. He was damage control officer and knew his way around the ship quite well, so he took us on a fascinating tour after dinner. Standing below decks and looking at steel armor 12 to 14 inches thick, it was difficult to believe that we were actually on board a ship that was floating in the water.

When I first started flying out of Mitchel Field, I was checked out in the B25 by an old classmate of mine from 43-J by the name of Eric Rheinhold. He had been at La Junta with me and shipped out with the rest of the guys when they were sent to Troop Carrier, but eventually got into B25s and stayed in when the war ended. It was a kick to see someone from the old "night fighter" bunch and we hoisted a few and told war stories after he checked me out.

One Saturday morning I was standing around Base Ops at Mitchel Field without any plane assignment when a pilot came up and asked me if I wanted to copilot for him in a B17G on a short flight up to Bangor, Maine and return. He was flying a general's B17 and his regular copilot couldn't make it. (The general wasn't going to be on the flight.) I told him I'd love to; he showed me how to pull up the wheels and milk up the flaps and off we went. After we got there and he had finished his business, he asked me if I would like to fly it on the return trip and I jumped at the chance. It was one of the sweetest planes I ever flew, almost took off and landed by itself. That was how I obtained the only four-engine time in my logbook.

In early May of 1948 I checked out in the Douglas A26, the

"big brother" to the A20 that I flew in combat. It was a great flying airplane, lots of power, and a joy to fly (though I would still rather have had the nimble little A20 for low-level strafing and skip-bombing). I flew to Chicago in an A26 on May 24th with only the crew chief along for the ride. On the return flight the next day, the weather was socked in along the entire half of the eastern U.S. and I filed a flight plan to La Guardia Field flying on top of the overcast, with an instrument approach at La Guardia. As we traveled east, the top of the overcast kept rising and by the time I was near La Guardia, I was at 14,000 feet, and again, no oxygen. I called in to Airway Traffic Control and was chagrined to learn that I was number fourteen to let down into La Guardia! There were planes stacked every thousand feet from the ground up. With all the crackling on the radio indicating thunderstorms in the area, and without a copilot to help, I decided discretion was the better part of valor and headed for my alternate destination at Rome, New York, which was CAVU (ceiling and visibility unlimited). So, the crew chief and I spent the night in Rome and flew on home to Mitchel Field the next day in good weather.

At the end of May we had completed our meteorology training and were assigned to various air bases across the country. The thing that was most unusual was that, with one exception, we were all given the assignments we had asked for. It was almost a truism in the military that you never got the assignment you asked for, so it was all the more surprising to learn that 54 out of the 55 had indeed received the assignments they had requested. (The one exception was the individual who had not had any overseas service and was sent to an overseas base.) The reason, of course, was that every air base in the country needed weather officers and so whichever place of assignment had been requested, a need existed.

Since I had requested Orchard Place Airport in Chicago (actually, Park Ridge, Illinois), that's where I was sent. I checked into the base and learned that they had no quarters for unmarried officers. Consequently, I ended up living at home with my parents and commuting 32 miles each way to the base. I flew AT6s and AT11s (the twin-engine Beechcraft) until February and then checked out in the A26 again (now designated the B26, since the Martin Marauder, the original B26, was dropped from service at the end of the war.) By this time the AT designation had also been discontinued and the trainers were designated simply T6, T11, etc. In April I checked out in the C46, the Curtis Commando, since we had a reserve Troop Carrier unit on the base. I can't say it was my favorite plane; it was a big lumbering beast with few redeeming features other than having a huge cargo hold for carrying large, bulky items. It was quite awkward to land and to taxi because, with its large fuselage and conventional landing gear (i.e., a tail wheel), the pilot and copilot sat so high off the ground and at such an angle that it was difficult to see the runway and taxiways.

I had one memorable flight in a B26, the night a friend and I were flying back from a trip to Omaha. The ceiling was about 1200 feet and the visibility a bare three miles. We were flying VFR (visual flight rules) which meant that we were not under Air Traffic Control (ATC) and had to make sure that we didn't get into the clouds. Occasionally, through breaks in the clouds, we could see thunderstorm activity off to the south of us, with much cloud-to-cloud lightning. We stayed on the airway and flew the beam, trying to keep the airway beacons in view as much as possible. Of course, after we passed over a beacon, we had to fly about seven miles before we could see the next one. It was a real sweat job, not knowing if the visibility would decrease or the ceiling lower so that we would have to go on instruments and get an emergency instrument clearance through ATC. Radio communication was not too clear that night and we weren't sure we'd even be able to contact them. It was a classic case for the famous "180-degree turn," but we doggedly kept on. Fortunately, the weather did not get any worse, and we got through O.K. but, once again, luck was on our side.

Another sweat job was the night I was flying back to Orchard Place after visiting my cousins in Wyandotte, Michigan. I was flying the single-engine T6 on a direct flight (VFR of course) from Wyandotte to Orchard Place. This took me directly across Lake Michigan. As I was crossing the lake, in the dark, and with lowering ceiling, I kept wondering why I had put myself into such a situation. The visibility and ceiling continued to decrease and I became painfully aware of the bind I was in. About the time I was ready to turn around and go back, I saw the famous "Lindy light" on top of one of the Chicago skyscrapers and was able to press on under minimum, but still VFR, conditions. Although it was only 50 miles across the lake and not 2000 miles, I had an inkling of how those intrepid pilots felt crossing the mighty Atlantic at night in small, single-engine airplanes. One tends to focus intently on the sound of the engine and anxiously scan the engine instruments at every opportunity.

The two longest flights I ever attempted in single-engine planes were the two trips I took from Orchard Place to Pensacola, Florida. My brother, Donald, was a naval aviation cadet in training there. In July of 1948 I flew down to see him in a T6, both to get in the flying time for my requirements and to have a visit with him. When I arrived and parked the plane, I walked into Base Operations in my flying suit and with my parachute slung over my shoulder and the O.O.D. (officer-of-the-deck) asked me which service I was in. I replied, "The Air Force." He said, "Which air force?" and I replied, "The

United States Air Force, of course." At that point we both realized that it was no longer the Army Air Force and the Navy Air Force, but the US Air Force, the Army, and the Navy.

It was a long flight, seven hours in the saddle, with two stops for refueling. I stayed with my brother overnight and we had a good visit. The next afternoon I flew back to Chicago, logging a couple of hours of night time before landing at my home base.

The second such flight was only two months later when I decided to fly down to Pensacola to bring him back to Chicago for a few days leave. I wasn't able to schedule the plane for an RON (remain overnight) so I had to fly down, pick him up, and return the same night. I didn't get off my forecasting shift until four in the afternoon, so it was about five when I got started. The weather was not great but believed to be VFR all the way. I had a few hours of daylight, but, by the time I got to Maxwell Field, Alabama for my second refueling stop, it was well past sunset. Moreover, weather conditions on the Gulf Coast were deteriorating, with ground fog forming at many of the coastal stations. Pensacola was still open and the six-hour forecast on the teletype was for no change. (I remember how many times I had sent that out myself because I just wasn't sure what would happen. Statistically speaking, in the absence of any information, the best forecast is "no change.") Unfortunately, in the real world, weather changes can be quite abrupt and unforeseen, as we well realize.

Nevertheless, I argued that the local forecaster was more familiar with eccentricities in the local weather than the rest of us were, and that I was willing to take a chance on his forecast. I finally got an instrument clearance to proceed to Pensacola with the understanding that it would be VFR when I arrived there. If not, I had to clear through ATC for an instrument letdown (something I was not enthusiastic about in a single-engine plane at night). I lucked out and the weather held, whereas practically every other station on the coast was socked in with ground fog. When I got there, I talked to the local forecaster and he explained that it was not an unusual situation, that frequently the coastal stations would be covered by ground fog but Pensacola would stay clear or be the last to fog over.

I picked up my brother and we headed north for the return trip. Maxwell Field and Scott Field stayed open and we had no problem until we got back to Chicago, shortly after sunrise. While I was approaching Orchard Place, I could see that the visibility was steadily declining in smoke and haze. I stayed on top of the haze layer (above 2000 ft the visibility was almost unlimited) and flew right over the field. Looking straight down, I could see the runway and called the tower for landing instructions. The tower operator replied that the last visibility reported for Orchard Place was two miles and I would have to get an instrument clearance to let down through the smoke and haze. By this time, I had fifteen hours in the saddle since I left the afternoon before and no sleep that night. I wasn't the slightest bit interested in an instrument approach. I asked the tower if there was any other traffic in the area and he replied that there wasn't. I explained that I was the station weather officer and that the visibility looked like it was improving and would he have an observer go out and check it. The observer did, sent out a special message that the visibility was three miles (so I could land VFR) and then sent out another message a few moments after I landed indicating that the visibility had again decreased to two miles. I was happy to be on the ground and thanked the observer for his perceptiveness in the matter...

In the summer of 1949 my life took a dramatic turn — for the better. My brother had finished his training and was home for a visit. One day, after he had been out in the car, he told me, "I saw Loraine Blanger out riding her bicycle and she looked great. I think I'll call her up for a date." She had been in school with Don and lived with an aunt just a couple of blocks from us, but I didn't know her and had never met her. My mother knew her grandmother and had suggested that I take her out some time, but a mother's recommendation to take out a girl is a kiss of death. No self-respecting and self-motivated young Air Force officer would even consider such a thing. Unfortunately (but fortunately for me) the remainder of my brother's leave was cancelled and he wasn't able to follow through on it.

During this same period, I had an accident in my neat 1949 red Oldsmobile convertible and it was in the shop for some body work. After Don left, I picked up the car from the shop and drove it home. It was a beautiful summer night and I was itching to go somewhere in my repaired convertible, so I asked my mother if she would like to go out for a ride. She suggested instead that I call up that girl Don had been interested in to see if she would like to go out for a ride. (I should explain at this point that I had been dating several girls but was disillusioned by all of them. They just didn't seem to be what I was looking for, although I wasn't sure what I was looking for, and nothing serious ever came of it.) Despite my mother's suggestion, I knew that my brother had good taste and that if he had been interested in Loraine Blanger, she might bear looking into. I called her up, explained who I was, and asked if she would like to go out for a ride. Since she knew my brother and had met my mother several times, she agreed. I picked her up and her eyes shined (lovely eyes, they were, too) at the red convertible parked out on the curb. We drove out to 87th and Western Avenue for a Rainbow ice cream cone and listened to Mozart on the radio. It was a splendid evening and we were well on the way to falling in love. A few weeks later we became engaged and set a wedding date for early in December. We were married on December 3rd (a rainy night in Chicago but there was sunshine in our hearts) and have been happily married now for more than fifty-two years. At the time we married I knew that I was due for an overseas assignment, so I requested assignment to any area in which my wife could join me in two or three months (which at that time was par for the course for Air Force dependents).

We had a fascinating eighteen-day honeymoon in our red convertible, making it as far as Taxco, Mexico before our time and money ran out, and we returned home to a little furnished three-room apartment on the west side of Chicago. On January 2nd, I went to Base Operations to schedule a T6 to take my new bride up for a flight. At that time, a pilot could take his wife up for a flight in an Air Force plane twice a year (as I recall) to build confidence (on her part, that is). However, the sergeant informed me that the provision authorizing such flights had not been included in the new Air Force regulations that had taken effect just the day before (January 1st) and that it could no longer be done. It was many years before I was able to take her up in a small plane with me at the controls, but that is another story.

Late in February 1950, I received information relative to my overseas assignment; it was devastating. I was being sent to the weather station at Dharan, Saudi Arabia — no dependents allowed! After all, this was no longer wartime; then, one didn't expect to have his dependents accompany him. It just seemed ridiculous to do this to a couple married only a few months; surely, there were some single officers who could be sent. When I was single, I would have jumped at the chance to go to a place like that and explore a part of the world I had never been to before, but as a newly married man it seemed like a cruel sentence, indeed. I started searching the regulations to see if there were some honorable way out of it, but nothing availed. I was committed and that was it. I was ordered to report to the Port of Aerial Embarkation (PAE) at Westover, Massachusetts on April 3, 1950. To emphasize the point, the orders stated "Officer's dependents will not accompany or join him at the PAE."

One day near the middle of March, I cleared the base at Orchard Place and drove home with a heavy heart. We were going to pack up and drive to Massachusetts in a day or two, where Loraine and I would part and she would return to Chicago. I arrived home at our small apartment and Loraine told me that Col. Bechtel had called me from Scott Field and gave me the operator number to return his call. We had only a weather detachment at Orchard Place. Our squadron headquarters were at Scott Field and the squadron commander was Lt. Col. Bechtel. I called the long distance operator and she put me through to him. His first words were, "Hornbeck, I've got some bad news for you." Migod, here I was getting ready to go to Dharan for at least a year without my bride of three months, and he's got bad news for me! He then informs me that he has orders to take two of the pilots in the squadron off of flying status, and I was picked to be one of them. It was my last day in the weather squadron; the following day I would be enroute to Westover and attached to the 1600th Air Embarkation Squadron. It was a neat solution for him — he fulfilled half of his quota and I would be gone from his command, probably forever. This was the final blow. The only reason I had gone back on active duty was to fly, and now they were taking that away from me as well!

I should explain that this was a concerted effort by Louis Johnson (Secretary of Defense) to cut expenses in the Air Force. At this time, one had to be very careful planning cross-country trips. Not all Air Force bases could provide fuel to transient aircraft and it was necessary to plan a flight so that stops could be made at air bases that would fuel transients. As part of the economies, there was a determined effort to reduce the number of pilots whose principal duties were non-flying (such as weather officers). Flying costs money and the fewer "unnecessary" flights, the better. Somehow, the thought of maintaining proficiency for pilots whose skills might be needed again was lost in the budget crisis. Each Air Force Command was given its share of reductions. We were in the Air Weather Service, under the Military Air Transport Service (MATS), and the quotas were passed right down the line to Wings and then Squadrons. And there I was, the man on the receiving end!

At this point I was about ready to swallow poison, cut my throat, and jump off a tall building. Almost off-handedly, Col. Bechtel said, "Of course, you can elect to be released from active duty." Catching me completely by surprise, I asked how I could be released from active duty. It all went back to the contract I had signed when I applied for active duty and meteorology training. I had agreed to serve at least four years after completion of training, but the army (which it still was at that time) agreed that I would be a pilot on flying status. In essence, they broke the contract, so I was free now to ask to be released from active duty. I was totally flabbergasted and told him that I would have to talk to my wife about this and would call him back.

We spent a couple of emotional hours exploring all of the aspects of the situation. Even though I had been looking for a way out, this hit us both pretty hard and we had to think it through. It was obvious to both of us that we were not really into military life — we were not comfortable with the Officers' Club set and the military ways of doing things, but had been willing to put up with it (on the part of both of us) for the sake of my being able to continue flying and pursuing a career as a weather officer. Without the flying, there just didn't seem to be any point in it.

I called Col. Bechtel back and told him that I wanted out. I explained to him that I had signed out of the base and was, in essence, enroute to the PAE, and asked him what I should do about being released from active duty. He told me to go back to the base the next day, sign in again, and orders would be cut to have me released. I did so, and on April 14th received orders transferring me to Chanute AFB, Illinois for discharge from military service on April 30th.

But not before I had one last, enjoyable cross-country flight. I had decided to go back to college to get a degree in chemistry and was interested in specializing in radiochemistry. Ever since they dropped the atom bomb at the end of the war, I had been intensely interested in nuclear physics and chemistry, and wanted to pursue further studies in the field. I thought about the possibility of attending the University of New Mexico, in Albuquerque, and I scheduled a T11 for a flight to Kirtland AFB. On March 22nd I took off with the crew chief, who needed flying time, in the right seat. The first leg of the flight was to Offut AFB in Omaha. The weather was not great and I had to file an IFR flight plan out of the Chicago area to fly in the clouds at 8000 ft. (I note in my flight record that our airport was now officially called O'Hare Field. It was no longer Orchard Place Airport). As we were proceeding on course at our assigned altitude, I noticed that we were picking up ice (still no deicers on the planes I flew). I called ATC to get a change in altitude to see if I could get out of the icing conditions. It was at that point that I realized how my life had changed. Never before in all of the similar situations I had been in did I ever give a thought to anyone on the ground. Sure, I was aware of my parents, and my brother and sister, and knew that if I crashed it would be a blow to them, but I never thought about it while I was flying. Now I found myself thinking of my wife and of the responsibility I had to her, and of how devastating it would be for her if I crashed, and suddenly my concerns were weightier than they ever had been before. After that experience, I was really glad that I decided to get out of the service. For the first time, I could empathize with the men who had shared wartime experiences with me and who did have wives and children back home waiting for them. One must be of stern stuff indeed, to know that, and to feel that, and still go on, nevertheless. But then in wartime, you have to.

We were able to change altitude and evade any further icing conditions and finally made it to Omaha without trouble. We went on to Lowry AFB at Denver and stayed overnight. The next day we went on to Kirtland AFB at Albuquerque. The weather was beautiful, but the air was rough, really rough. We had a passenger that we picked up at Lowry, a young soldier who was late getting back from leave and needed a ride to ABQ. He was not accustomed to flying and suffered miserably from airsickness as the T11 tossed like a cork in an ocean storm. I asked him several times if I should turn around and go back, but he was so determined not to end up AWOL that he insisted I go on. (There wasn't any stable air that day at any altitude I could get to in that plane, so we just had to tough it out.) After two-and-a-half hours of bouncing, we arrived at Kirtland without incident, and no one in the history of flight was happier to get on the ground than our passenger.

My first impression of the area was not encouraging. We checked in to the transient quarters and I noticed the windows of the room I was in were nailed shut. (It was on the windy side of the building.) Despite this, I noticed a neat little ridge about a quarter of an inch high of very fine sand that ran along the window sill that had blown in through the cracks in the window frame. Fine dust was everywhere, in spite of efforts to keep the place cleaned up. After looking around Albuquerque, visiting the campus and the people in the Radiochemistry Department, I decided that was not the place for me. The next day we flew home, stopping only in Kansas City to refuel.

My last flight in the Air Force was on April 12th. I flew a T11 to Scott AFB and back for my last official visit to Squadron Headquarters. I have no recollections of the visit but I believe that I thanked Col. Bechtel for giving me the opportunity to get out of the service. If I didn't, I should have. On April 30th, I was discharged at Chanute AFB.

I returned to the University of Chicago to continue my studies in chemistry. Loraine went back to work in her old job as a typist in the telephone company to supplant my meager GI Bill allotment. Ironically, only a few weeks after I was discharged, we were at war again, in Korea. I did not volunteer for anything, having given up the military as a career, and was determined to make a career for myself in chemistry and to share my life with my wife and, eventually, our two lovely daughters.

Over the succeeding years, I flew occasionally as a civilian (having qualified for a civilian single- and multi-engine commercial rating,) but it wasn't the same as military flying. A Cessna 172 or 182 is pretty tame stuff compared to a P38 or an A20. In addition, civilian flying was too expensive a hobby for me to participate in by myself. As I mentioned earlier, I did get Loraine up in a 182 several years later, but it was white knuckles all the way. Because of a persistent claustrophobia (which is no big deal except in a crowded elevator) she is not comfortable in a small plane, but has no problem in modern jet aircraft. (One of my principal regrets concerning my short military career is that I didn't have the opportunity to check out in jets.)

After graduation from the University of Chicago with a B.S. degree in chemistry, I was able to pursue my civilian career at a number of different laboratories. I did research in the analytical chemistry of plutonium and uranium at the K-25 gaseous diffusion plant in Oak Ridge in 1951-2 and at Argonne Laboratory in 1954; developed a pilot plant for the production of calcium pantothenate (a B vitamin) at Chemlek Laboratories in Worth, IL in 1953; worked on the nuclear-powered seaplane project at the Martin Company in Baltimore from 1955 to 1957, which included a one-year stint as a loaned employee doing research on radiation damage to plastics at the Oak Ridge National Laboratory X-10 plant; did research on radiation-induced chemical reactions at Industrial Reactors Laboratories (IRL), Plainsboro, N.J. 1958-1962; and finally ended up as a radiochemist at Lawrence Livermore Laboratory, CA, where I have been since 1962. I retired from full-time service in 1982 and have been a part-time consultant and Laboratory Associate for the past twenty years.

My Brother Donald in VP-22 (1950)

My brother became a naval aviator and stayed in the Navy until he retired as a commander with thirty years of service. He, too, went into multi-engine flying and flew a variety of patrol bombers and transports. For a while he was flying with MATS and also flew radar picket in EC121 "Super Connies" from Iceland to Scotland and back during the period when we relied on those planes to close holes in our distant early warning radar net.

He retired in 1975 to Chula Vista, California so we were able to exchange visits over the years. He died on October 8, 2000 and is sorely missed. He, too, was one "who loved the vastness of the sky."

Sitting at this computer, in 2002, at the age of 79, with corrected vision and impaired hearing, I feel that I have been describing someone else's experiences, a different Robert F. Hornbeck, young, capable, and almost unreal to me now. But the memories are there, the experiences were real, and I am thankful that I have had the opportunity to write about them.

EPILOGUE

In late September 1988, I attended the 40th reunion of the 312th Bomb Group held in Harlingen, Texas. It was the first such reunion I had attended and it was particularly well timed. I was enroute to a meeting of the Foreign Weapons Evaluation Working Group to be held on October 2nd and 3rd at Cocoa Beach, Florida and was able to stop on the way to attend the reunion. The reunions were held every year at different locations, mostly in the East, and this was the first one I had known about.

Harlingen was a particularly interesting location for the reunion because it is the home of the Confederate Air Force, a private organization with the best collection of World War II military aircraft (that are still in flying condition) in the world today. All of us looked forward to seeing the many well-known WWII planes in the collection, particularly the Douglas A20G, which we had all flown. Unfortunately, the week before the reunion a fierce hurricane traveled through the Gulf of Mexico, headed directly for Harlingen. All of the planes in flyable condition except the A20 were evacuated to San Antonio, safely out of the path of the storm. I'm sure that the A20, too, would have been evacuated at the last minute, if it had been necessary.

Harlingen was spared when the storm veered to the north, but none of the planes had returned to their home base by the time of our reunion. Nevertheless, we were able to see the A20, climb up on it, take pictures, etc. Then a fellow by the name of Max Gardner, an A20 pilot from WWII, came out, climbed into the cockpit, started the engines, and took off on a short demonstration flight. You could almost see the goose pimples form on the old 312th Bomb Group pilots at the sound of the Wright-Cyclone R-2600s revving up and we thoroughly enjoyed watching him taxi out, take off, make a low pass down the runway, and land. For most of us, it had been 43 years since we had been that close to an A20 that could fly; it certainly was the high point of our reunion.

I met a few of the men I had flown with back in 1945, Wayne Roth, Murray Yates, and Ed Oldham. Many of the attendees had been in the group earlier than I and had left the group before I joined it, including the man who had been the much-respected group commander throughout most of the war, Col. Robert Strauss. The weekend following our reunion (Oct. 8th and 9th) was a big one for the Confederate Air Force. They were having their annual air show, at which they have everything flyable in the air. They stage mock battles and really put on a great show of WWII aircraft. I was surprised to read a small item in the Sunday SF Chronicle that a vintage twin-engine airplane crashed during the air show on Saturday. It was the A20 that we had seen and it had been flown by Max Gardner, who died in the crash. It turned out that he'd had severe coronary arteriosclerosis and had suffered a massive heart attack while flying in the air show. Fortunately, no one else was in the plane at the time. It was a great loss, and now I don't know of any A20s still flying, though a few are in various air museums around the country.

One couple I met at the reunion in Harlingen was from Sonoma,

California: Bob and Carolyn Spencer. They were very helpful and introduced me to many of the old-timers that I had not known. Bob was a pilot in the 387th Squadron and left the group to return to the States just a month or two before I got there. Bob hosted the 41st reunion held the following year (1989) in San Francisco. By advertising widely, he was able to bring in several more members who had not previously attended reunions. Among them were "Red" Cleveland, Eddie Bretch, Glenn Randolph, and John Happy, all of whom I had flown with and remembered; in addition, Col. Wells, the group C.O. when I was in the group, attended for the first time. He retired as a three-star general. All told, there were thirty-six pilots present, including Col. Strauss and General Wells. The reunion was held at the Marines' Memorial Club in San Francisco and was very well done. Bob worked hard to put together a good program and it was quite successful. Sadly, Bob died a few years ago.

Recently, I was talking to a person by the name of Jim Hassberger, who is in the same division I am in at the lab (LLNL). He has an office just a few doors down the hall from mine. He was telling me that his father was a navigator on a B24 in the SWPA (Southwest Pacific Area) during WWII. They had a copilot on the crew who ended up leaving the crew to go into A20s and Jim thought his name was Frank Happy. It turned out that Frank is a brother of John Happy and that they were both flying A20s in the SWPA, although Frank was in a different Bomb Group. Another item for "it's a small world."

We did have a pair of brothers in the group, Marion and Cyrus Hershberger. Marion was in the 387th squadron with me and transferred to the 388th, as I did, when the 387th was converted to B32s. I don't remember which squadron Cyrus was in. It seemed unusual to have two brothers flying the same type of plane and in the same Bomb Group.

My web site dedicated to the 312th Bomb Group contains many more photos from that time, including some taken on combat missions. It can be accessed at:

http://rfhornbeck.home.comcast.net

There are links to my other web sites with more photos of my personal flying experiences during and after the war.

Loraine and I in Yosemite Nov. 1998

Revising History

Every year, around the anniversary of the bombing of Hiroshima and Nagasaki, groups of people appear outside the gates of Livermore Laboratory, protesting the dropping of the atomic bombs that ended the war. They even question the morality of President Truman and others in his administration who claim justification for the mass killings as necessary to "save the lives of our boys," implicitly suggesting that this was not a justifiable reason. Their claim that Japan was already defeated and ready to surrender is not borne out by the facts. There were people in the Japanese government who were interested in ending the conflict, but the militarists retained an iron grip on the government and were not the slightest bit interested in pursuing peace. Although facing the reality of military defeat, they still had an army of three million men and over 9,000 planes that could be used in Kamikaze attacks on the invasion forces. To the militarists, surrender was not an option.

As we have seen, the closer that the Allied Forces came to the home islands, the fiercer and deadlier became the defense. In the battle for Okinawa, U.S. military casualties totaled almost 50,000 with 12,250 dead or missing. Thirty-six U.S. ships were sunk and 386 more damaged by Kamikaze attacks. An estimated 110,000 Japanese were killed and about 80,000 Okinawa civilians were killed or committed suicide at the urging of the Japanese military. How could anyone seriously believe that our invasion of the main islands would not have resulted in far greater casualties? Projecting from the Okinawa experience, military planners estimated as many as a million Allied casualties from the invasion of the home islands. These are the facts that Truman and his administration had to confront when they faced their decision to drop the bomb.

It is true, and deplorable, that 70,000-80,000 civilians died in the Hiroshima bombing and another 40,000 in Nagasaki. To put this in context, on the night of March 9-10, 1945 three hundred thirty-four B29s covered Tokyo with ordinary incendiary bombs that killed more than 83,000 civilians and wounded 41,000. (Similar casualties were observed in the disastrous fire-bombing of Dresden, Germany.) Unfortunately, that is the nature of modern war. Five major Japanese cities (Tokyo, Yokohama, Kobe, Osaka, and Nagoya) were virtually destroyed; B29s were concentrating on their secondary cities with fifty-four thousand tons of incendiaries dropped between the end of June and the middle of August, and still the Japanese would not surrender. It really did take two atomic bombs to bring them to the point of "unconditional surrender" as had been defined by President Roosevelt. Anyone who doesn't recognize this is refusing to face the facts.

I have no quarrel with people who have a conviction that nuclear weapons should be banned. I would be happy indeed to live in a world in which there were no such weapons of mass destruction (as we have heard so much about lately). However, I firmly believe that without our nuclear arsenal and the policy of "mutual assured destruction" (M.A.D.) during the past fifty years, we would have been in a major conventional war with the Soviet Union at some time in that period, a war that would have been disastrous both for the free world and the Soviet Union. The nuclear genie is firmly out of the bottle and no matter how desperately we try, we're not going to get it back in the bottle. The best that we can hope for is that sanity will prevail and that no one who has nuclear weapons will use them except as a deterrent, and that those who would be insane enough to use them never have access to them.

APPENDIX. EXTRACTS FROM MY LOGBOOK/DIARY

****

In order to preserve both the accuracy of the account and to retain the flavor of the time, I reproduce here extracts from the personal logbook/diary that I kept during this period. As you can see, I kept track of which plane I flew, the type and amount of bomb load, the target, and observations from the mission itself. Comments are reproduced exactly as they were written except, occasionally, for clarity, words are written out that were abbreviated in the logbook.

Anything that is given in the form (Note: ...) represents an explanatory remark or comment from the present time; any other parentheses are from the logbook. Bomb types are summarized as follows: PD for parachute-retarded demolition bombs; PF for parachute-retarded fragmentation bombs; FG for fragmentation bombs; FC for fragmentation cluster bombs; GP for general-purpose demolition bombs; Np for napalm bombs.

Where I indicate that the load consisted of 6X250 demos, it means that on low-level strikes we carried four parademos in the bomb bay and one free-fall demo on each wing. For obvious reasons, parachute-retarded bombs were always carried in the bomb bay; they were armed when the parachute was pulled out of its container as the bomb hit the slipstream. These bombs usually had 3-4 second delay fuses. Bombs dropped from wing racks usually had 12-15 second delay fuses. Since we were so low when the bombs hit the ground, it was essential that they not detonate on impact, hence the delayed fusing. I have photos showing bombs bouncing up almost as high as the aircraft after they had hit the ground. If the bomb load is shown as 14X100, it means that we had two 100-lb bombs attached to each rack in the bomb bay and a cluster of three on each wing.

The one exception was the 23-lb parafrag dropped from multiple racks within the bomb bay. This small, but effective, bomb had a large nose plug shaped like a big golf tee and was armed when the parachute pulled out. The bomb would detonate if the tee hit anything, even a twig of a tree, since they were most effective when they went off in the air. They were guaranteed to put a high-speed fragment of shrapnel in every square yard at a distance of 50 yards. We carried 80 of them in these special bomb racks and they were automatically released 1/3rd of a second apart. We dropped these while we were flying side-by-side (line abreast) at about 200 feet of altitude as we traversed the target area. At 300 mph, this would put one every 50 yards, longitudinally, and about the same distance apart laterally. We carried 2100 rounds of .50-cal ammunition for the six forward-firing guns in the nose (350 rounds per gun) and several hundred rounds for the turret guns. At 1/2 pound per cartridge+link, this was over half a ton of ammunition.

Mission #1 was on March 23, 1945. Flying A20G, serial no. 398, bomb load 4X300 GP, mission time 3 hr 15 min; target Wewak, New Guinea; flight of six planes. Rifkin (number 3 position) turned back due to engine trouble. (Note: this was a common problem with these old war-weary aircraft.) Lost second element. (Note: they literally got lost but made it back to the base.) Nothing sighted. No visible damage.

#2 on 3/25: A20G 398, 4X300 GP, 3 hr 40 min, Wewak: flight of six, Rothgeber turned back.. I moved from No. 5 position in rear element to No. 2 position in front element. Unable to reach primary target inland due to weather so struck at targets on coast.

Sighted two small huts.

#3 on 4/1: A20G 244, 4X260 FG, 4 hr 15 min, six-plane flight, target a village 20 mi. S of Dagua, New Guinea. Supposed to drop from 3500' on wing of B25, then strafe. Lead ship and Harris (#2) turned back. Flew TOVC (top of overcast) at 6000' to target, let down to 1000', did not sight B25s. Flew 20 minutes past target, flubbed around for 10-15 minutes, came back over the mountains and building cumulus clouds. (Note: we salvoed our bombs in the jungle to aid in climbing up over the mountains and the rapidly rising cumulus. All in all, this mission was an exercise in frustration.)

#4 on 4/2: A20G 244, 4X260 FG, 4 hr 39 min, six-plane flight, same target as previous day. Woody and McCormick turned back. Oakley went on with Harris, Rifkin, and myself. Dropped bombs in train on lead B25 from 3500', results unobserved. Peeled off after bombing run, made several strafing runs on many huts along the river.

(Note: This ended our tour at the CRTC. With the exception of the 4/12 orientation flight, which was out of Lingayen, from here on our missions were in the 312th Bomb Group, 387th Bomb Squadron, operating out of the dirt strip at Floridablanca, 10 mi. S of Clark Field, Luzon.)

4/12 B25J 961: Local flight for orientation. Fired at over Baguio; also flew over Manila. (Note: this was the first time I had seen AA bursts; the targets we had attacked in New Guinea didn't have any serviceable 90-mm guns left and only offered automatic weapons and rifle fire from the ground.)

#5 on 4/20: A20G, (tail marking "J"), 4X250 PD, twelve-plane flight, 3 hr 50 min, target Infanta - strafed and bombed houses on the edge of town supposedly holding Japanese troops and supplies; several direct hits.

#6 0n 4/22: A20G (+), 4X500GP, 3 hr 50 min, Balete Pass (primary target) socked in and went on to hit secondary (Pattao). Dropped on wing of B25 from 3000'. Hit ammo dump, all bombs in target area; heavy explosions and much smoke.

#7 on 4/24: A20G (V), 8X100 PD, 2 hr 20 min, target Lampong - troop and supply concentrations. Bad target, had to hop over steep hill to strafe and bomb in ravine with high hills on both sides.

(8) on 4/26: A20G J, 2X250 PD, 20 min, had to abort; left landing gear strut collapsed on takeoff and would not retract. (Note: we had been ordered to bring back bombs and not salvo them because of short supplies. I had to land downwind with a full load of fuel, bombs, and ammo. I came in hot and wasn't about to stop when I got to the end of the strip. A GI in a truck coming down the road that crossed the end of the strip stopped just before he got in front of me. I could see the surprised expression on his face as I went rolling by him at about 50 mph. I crossed the road and brought the plane to a stop in the fields beyond. It was quite fortunate that there were no ditches or embankments on the sides of the road and that the ground was hard and dry. I was able to turn the plane around and taxi back to the landing strip without any trouble. No damage was done but I sure had some tight sphincter muscles taxiing in...)

#8 on 4/27: A20G (T) 4X250 PD , 3 hr, target San Pablo - Major Miller leading the squadron, hit to left of target on first pass. Dropped two on huts, two in field because no targets visible, then made second pass and strafed town. Harris (flying with Sharkey) was cut on face when ricochet hit turret and splintered the Plexiglass.

#9 on 4/28: A20G (+) 4X250 PD, 4 hr, target 10 mi. S of Ballesteros, Capt. Svore leading (386th Squadron). L-5 spotted target along west bank of Cagayan River. Dropped bombs and strafed on first pass (south to north) made two more strafing runs north to south. Hit several huts, started small fires. Sighted 50' pole by which Japs strung cable across river. Was hit in right side of fuselage about 12-14" below seat by Jap .25 cal. slug. Made hole about 1" on a side, stopped inside nose wheel well.

#10 on 5/2: A20G (R) 80X23 PF, 2 hr 10 min, target Diadi - concentration of 1500 Japanese troops, 3 tanks, 3 105-mm guns; several on mission claimed to have seen one tank and several trucks. Target surrounded by hills with very low broken cumulus clouds. Only 4 racks released due to mechanical failure. Sighted nothing but target was very well covered with strafing and frags.

5/3: B25J (961) FB-Tanuan(Leyte)-FB Two good missions today and I had to go on a "fat-cat" with Tieman. Hard luck! Got some sheets and pajamas at Tacloban QM.

#11 on 5/5: A20G (R) 6x250 demos, 2 hr 30 min, target Solano - troops and supplies quartered in fair-sized town. Good target. Lead ship (Tranchitella) went right down "Main Street". Many good buildings were on my side and I strafed and bombed them with good results. My right wing bomb failed to release. (Note: this occasioned another tense landing, wondering if it would fall off and explode when I landed; it didn't.)

#12 on 5/6: A20G (I) 6X250 demos, 2 hr 30 min, target Lattu

- troop and supply concentrations on edge of town. Capt.Svore leading 386th. Bad weather all the way but we got down through a hole. Hit target with good bomb coverage. Nothing sighted but an old church that received several direct hits. (On Sunday, too.)

#13 on 5/9: A20G (B from the 386th) 4X500 FC, 2 hr 5 min, target trail NE of Baguio, Mt. Kamalkatan - troop concentration. Maj. Miller led. Dropped from 4000' on Group B25 (961). Target area well covered.

#14 on 5/10: A20G (W from the 386th) 6X250 PD, 2 hr 5 min, target area N of Infanta - supposed to hit artillery positions in mts. with Infanta as secondary. Circled 45 min over primary, unable to contact ground station, went on to secondary. Made two passes, didn't see anything but scattered huts. Took off and landed on new strip. Wonderful. Smooth and long.

#15 on 5/11: A20G (B from the 386th) 4X250 PD and 6X100 Np (two bundles of three on wing racks), 4 hr 20 min, target Paranum - 850 Japanese troops quartered in town and nearby wooded area. Col. Wells led the group (all four squadrons)... Bad weather all the way up and back. Had to go by sea and cut through mountain passes several times. Hit town west to east, dropped bombs and strafed. Circled back and made strafing run (south to north) along wooded area. Observed several huts blazing fiercely.

#16 on 5/16: A20G (L) 4X250 PD, 6X100 Np, 2 hr 35 min, target San Juan- Jap troops and sympathizers in town and adjacent fields. Capt. Svore led all 4 squadrons (36 planes). Made long strafing run hitting many huts. Toggled all bombs in target area. Many fires started, smoke rose to 3000'. Target completely covered. Sighted Jap machine gun but was out of ammo and unable to strafe.

#17 on 5/17: A20G (R) 4X250 PD, 6X100 Np, 2 hr 30 min, target Mankayan - mining camp on side of hill. Maj. Miller led. I took off as spare and took Pritchard's place when he dropped out.

#18 on 5/22: A20G (+) 6X250 FG, 2 hr 20 min, target Gubano - dropped medium altitude on wing of B25. Uneventful, dropped all bombs, sighted nothing.

#19 on 5/25: A20G (J) 14X100 demo, 2 hr 20 min, target Santa Fe - close ground support in Balete Pass. 192 fighters hit first with napalm tanks. Artillery did excellent job of spotting target with white phosphorous. Fighters covered target thoroughly with fire bombs. Flames rose 150-200' in the air, smoke to 7000'. Target was surrounded by 3000 to 4000-foot hills. Very hard to get into. Went in after smoke lifted and hit Japanese strongpoint on side of hill. Mission very successful. (Could not strafe because of proximity of our troops.)

#20 on 5/27: A20G (R) 80X23 PF, 2X100 Np, 3 hr 30 min, target Piggitan -troop bivouac area in woods along Cagayan River. Capt. Svore led group, Steve led us. Strafed area and covered with frags. Nothing sighted, small fires started.

#21 on 5/28: A20G (R) 6X260 FG, 2 hr 30 min, target Kabiten - troops in wooded areas in mountains. Dropped from 9000 ft. on B25. Nothing sighted, mission uneventful.

#22 on 5/29: A20H (O) 80X23 PF, 2 hr 15 min, target Santiago - troops and supplies along Highway 5 on outskirts of town. Strafed and bombed huts in wooded area west of town. Several fires started. Human interest -- on strafing run along a hedgerow, I passed over 35-40 civilians lying side-by-side against the hedgerow, arms over heads, and huddled together for protection. They sure looked helpless. P.S. I don't think I hit any of them.

#23 on 5/30: A20G (+) 14X100 demo, 2 hr 30 min, target Echague - troops bivouacked in woods S of airstrip. Capt. Stephens led, I flew with 388th. Made good strafing run, all bombs hit in target area which was well covered.

#24 on 5/31: A20G (Y) 6X250 demo, 2 hr 30 min, target Balete Pass - close ground support against Japanese strongpoint. Steve led, ground control spotted target with WP. Had to dive steeply down side of mountain to hit target (indicated air speed 310 mph). Nothing sighted but fires.

#25 on 6/1: A20G (+) 6X250 demo, 2 hr 30 min, ground support. L-5 spotted target with smoke at bottom of canyon. Had to dive steeply (over 310 mph). Bomb pattern good, target well covered. Had full throttle and rpm trying to climb out. Could not turn with flight leader, had to make 270-deg turn to gain more altitude. Close call but got out OK.

#26 on 6/2: A20G (J) 6X250 demo, 2 hr, target Baguio area (10 mi NE). Close ground support. L-5 spotted target on top of ridge with WP. Hit from N to S, strafed and dropped all bombs directly on target. Ground station praised our work highly.

#27 on 6/2: A20H (K) 6X250 demo, 2 hr, target Balete Pass - close ground support. WP shells outlined target in densely wooded area on side of mountain. Strafed and dropped all bombs in target area.

6/4 Flew courier down to Tacloban (B25). Dropped off at

Mindoro and saw Blue, Woody, Sparks, Rex Morris. Stayed long enough to win nine pesos in a pinochle game.

6/5 Had skip-bombing practice against shipwreck this morning. Had to use emergency gear release to get left wheel down on "R."

#28 on 6/5: A20G (J) 14X100 demo, 2 hr 30 min, target Angadanan - hit Japanese troop and supply concentrations. Made long strafing run hitting many huts and starting fires. Target area well covered with bombs.

#29 on 6/6: A20H (J 053) 14X100 demo, 3 hr, target Viga - troop and supply concentrations in town. Made good strafing run many huts. Dropped all bombs in target area. Several large fires observed.

#30 on 6/6: A20G (P) 14X100 demo, 2 hr 45 min, target Viga - hit troop bivouac area south of town along river. Had to release fuselage bombs on other side of river on small town because I was crowded off target.

#31 on 6/7: A20G (F) 14X100 demo, 2 hr, target Ipo area - ground support in conjunction with napalm attack by fighters. Strafed and bombed target with no visible results.

#32 on 6/10: A20G (L) 6X250 demo, 2 hr 55 min, target Santiago - ground support. Our troops have pushed through Balete Pass and are advancing up the Cagayan valley. Strafed and bombed target with no visible results.

#33 on 6/11: A20G (+) 6X250 demo, 2 hr 10 min, target Ipo area - ground support in mountains. Smoke was off target and we made two dry runs over our own troops. On third pass we dropped all bombs directly on target.

6/12 Flew down to Mindoro twice today with Schissler in the group C47. Got 5:35 copilot time. It's easy to fly and all in all a pretty fair aircraft.

#34 on 6/13 A20G (+) 6X250 demo, 3 hr 5 min, target Tuguegarao - hit ammo and gas dump in wooded area near town. Nothing sighted, had good buzz job.

#35 on 6/15: A20H (C) 4X250PD, 6X100 Np, 4 hr, target vicinity Ilagan - hit troop and supply concentrations. Sighted several small huts and some fires started.

#36 on 6/15: A20G (V) 4X250 PD, 6Z100 Np, 2 hr 35 min, target vicinity Ilagan - hit ammo and gas dump. Large fires started, one heavy explosion observed. Smoke rose to 3000'.

6/16 Flew down to Mindoro in C47 again, with Tieman. Saw Bufkin for a few minutes. His outfit is changing to A26s any day now.

#37 on 6/17: A20H (O) 8X100 demo, 6X100 Np, 3 hr 5 min, target Namabbalan - hit supply dump in wooded area. Several fires.

#38 on 6/19: A20H (I) 4X250 demo, 3 hr, target Tuguegarao - hit troop and supply concentrations on S edge of town. Several fires started. Guerrillas cross Cagayan tonight and commence drive to the east.

#39 on 6/19: A20H (M) 14X100 Np, 3 hr, target Tuguegarao -

same area as this morning. More of the black cylindrical objects observed to come up at planes. Nobody has been hit by one yet. A gunner saw one explode in the air.

#40 on 6/22: A20G (N) 14X100 Np, 2 hr 15 min, target Hucab - ground support. Bombed and strafed concentration of Japanese troops on ridge alongside road.

#41 on 6/23: A20H (H) 14X100 Np, 3 hr 30 min, target Hucab - hit Japanese troops dug in gully just half a mile southeast of yesterday's target. Made one dry run (Note: to make sure we didn't hit our own troops).

#42 on 6/24: A20H (K) 8X100 PD, 6X100 Np, 4 hr 25 min, target Tuguegarao - unable to contact Bygone ground controller, went up to Bunny and hit concentration along river north of Tuguegarao. (Note: "Bygone" and "Bunny" were code names for the ground controllers that we contacted for target information. These were combat pilots stationed with the ground troops to direct us into the target.)

#43 on 7/20: A20G (O) 14X100 demo, 3 hr 50 min, target Mankayan area - ground support with guerrilla troops in mountains. Cub spotted target with WP. Lots of bad weather.

#44 on 8/15: Schissler and I took off in the C47 for Okinawa at 0815. At 0830 I tuned in WVTM on the radio compass and we heard the announcement that the war was over!

Bibliography

Bodie, Warren M. *The Lockheed P-38 Lightning.* Hiawassee: Widewing Publications, 1991.

Costello, John. *The Pacific War 1941-1945.* New York: Quill, 1982.

Crosswind, Class book for the class of 43-J. Mira Loma Flight Academy, 1943.

Gailey, Harry A. *The War in the Pacific.* Novato: Presidio Press, 1997.

Hand Book, *The Curtis Standard JN4-D Military Tractor.* Buffalo: Curtis Aeroplane & Motor Car Corporation, 1918.

Hess, William N. *A-20 Havoc at War.* New York: Charles Scribner's Sons.

Matt, Paul R. *Historical Aviation Album, Volume XV.* Temple City, 1977.

Maupin, Robert N. *Flying Cadets of WWII.* New York: McGraw-Hill, 1999.

Pace, Steve. *B-25 Mitchell.* Osceola: Motorbooks Int. Publishers & Wholesalers, 1994.

Pilot's Manual for Lockheed P-38 Lightning. Milwaukee: Aviation Publications, 1972.

Pilot's Manual for Northrop P-61 Black Widow. Milwaukee: Aviation Publications, 1973.

Rust, Ken R. *Fifth Air Force Story.* Terra Haute: Sun Shine House, 1973.

Silver Wings, Class book for the class of 43-J. Williams Field, AZ, 1943.

Sturzebecker, Russell L. *The Roarin' 20s.* Kennet Square: KNA Press, Inc., 1976.

Printed in the United States
19150LVS00001B/424-435